Advance Praise f | | barcode | | T0056869

"This concise book is a potent antidote to the apocalypse meme. Thank you, John Michael Greer, for showing how the apocalypse virus isn't fatal, but chronic."

—Douglas Rushkoff, author of *Life Inc.*
and *Program or Be Programmed*

"This sweeping survey of apocalyptic thought during the last three and a half millennia is written with erudition and sprinkled with humor. John Michael Greer seamlessly weaves the threads of religious/mystical and secular/revolutionary apocalypticism—from the best-known exemplars to the delightfully obscure. I am confident this notable work will be around long after winter solstice 2012, continuing to serve the reader with its important explication of this critical subject and pointing the way to associated literature for further study."

—James Wasserman, author of *The Temple of Solomon: From Ancient Israel to Secret Societies*

"It was important for somebody to take on this faux-religious madness, this yearning for the death of our planet. Hooray for John Michael Greer for skewering the lot of them on his acerbic pen! From the artificial counting of the dates of the end of the world to the last big bout of robbing people of their money, hopes, and religious beliefs, Greer tracks this male madness faithfully. This seems to be a very American obsession, the end of days, profitable to those who spread it, a doom to those who drink their Kool-Aid."

—Z Budapest, author of
Celestial Wisdom for Every Year of Your Life and
The Holy Book of Women's Mysteries

"The perfect hangover cure for the day before the day after the day the world didn't end."

—Lon Milo DuQuette, author of
The Key to Solomon's Key

"*Apocalypse Not* is a riotous romp through the history of the human imagination. Mr. Greer takes us around the world and across millennia, from sacred to secular, to bring us this tribute to the limitless creativity and tenacious desire of the human heart despite all odds. The book details our human need to seek a utopian world, a world available only to the worthy by a trial that makes it worthwhile. He proves it's not the Armageddon that draws us to embrace the idea of a pending apocalypse, but the dream of the paradise that lies beyond. Reading this book will make you laugh at human folly and cry at its consequences, as you meet some of the most colorful figures in history."

—Jeff Hoke, author of *The Museum of Lost Wonder*

"If peddling flesh is the world's oldest profession, John Michael Greer makes a good case that peddling fear is not too far behind. *Apocalypse Not* lucidly spells out how social upheaval—as well as plain old boredom and frustration—have always inspired fantasies of The Great Reboot, when lions will lay down with lambs, streets will be paved with gold, and lowly stock boys will become lofty CEOs. This book explains the hows and whys of such grand fantasies throughout history and how often they seem to come to grief. Armageddon through to you?"

—Christopher Knowles, author of
The Secret History of Rock 'n' Roll and *Our Gods Wear Spandex*

"Look no further than *Apocalypse Not* for your explanation of 2012 end times, apocalypse memes, starlore, and pseudo-philosophers in man's rich history of end-of-the-world obsessions."

—Nick Belardes, author of *Random Obsessions*

"*Apocalypse Not* breaks open the doomsday clock, revealing all its cogs and inner workings. The end isn't near: it's Greer."

—Clint Marsh, author of *The Mentalist's Handbook*

APOCALYPSE
NOT

APOCALYPSE
NOT

EVERYTHING YOU KNOW
ABOUT 2012, NOSTRADAMUS
AND THE RAPTURE IS WRONG

John Michael Greer

Viva
EDITIONS

Published in the United States by Viva Editions,
an imprint of Cleis Press, Inc.,
2246 Sixth Street, Berkeley, California 94710.

Printed in the United States.
Cover design: Scott Idleman/Blink
Cover photograph: Chad Baker/Getty Images
Text design: Frank Wiedemann
First Edition.
10 9 8 7 6 5 4 3 2 1

Trade paper ISBN: 978-1-936740-00-0
E-book ISBN: 978-1-936740-05-5

Library of Congress Cataloging-in-Publication Data

Greer, John Michael.
Apocalypse not : a history of the end of time / John Michael Greer.
-- 1st ed.
p. cm.
Includes bibliographical references and index.
ISBN 978-1-936740-00-0 (pbk. : alk. paper)
1. Eschatology. 2. Apocalyptic literature--History and criticism.
3.Prophecies. 4. End of the world. I. Title.
BL501.G74 2011
202'.3--dc23

2011024800

CONTENTS

COUNTING DOWN TO THE APOCALYPSE

I n the old Chinese calendar it will be the ninth day of the eleventh lunar month, at the end of the period Daxue, "Great Snow," in the year of the Monkey 4649. Muslims around the world will call it Yaum al-Juma, the eighth day of Safar in the year 1434 after the Hegira, while the Hindu calendar gives the date as Sukravara, the seventh day of Margashirsha in the year 1934 of the Śakya era and 5113 of the Kali Yuga, the last and darkest age of this cycle of the world.

In the Julian calendar of ancient Rome, the same date would have been the sixth day before the Ides of December in the year 2765 from the founding of Rome, while the

French revolutionary calendar, that weird and almost forgotten offspring of Enlightenment rationalism, would have called that day Primidi in the first decade of the month of Nivose in the year of the Revolution 221. The ancient Egyptians would have called it the sixth day of Pachon, though they would have had a hard time putting a number to the year—Egyptian years were counted from the start of the current pharaoh's reign, and this sixth of Pachon will come more than two millennia after the last Lord of the Two Lands went to dwell with his divine father Osiris in the heavens of Amentet. The Western world will call it Friday, December 21, 2012.

More than a thousand years ago, the astronomers and mathematicians of another ancient people worked out this same date in their own calendar, and set in motion a chain of events that made their calculations a topic of fear and fascination across much of the world today. They were the Mayans, and to them the date in question was 4 Ahau 3 Kankin 13.0.0.0.0—the end of the thirteenth and final baktun of the current great cycle of time, and, according to a widespread modern belief, the end of the world.

According to claims you can find retailed at great length in an abundance of books these days, the ancient Mayans were unlike any other people in history. They appeared suddenly out of nowhere thousands of years ago, complete with a culture and a technology that was unrelated to those of their neighbors and showed no signs whatsoever of gradual development over time, and they vanished just as suddenly a little more than a thousand years ago, abandoning their great stone cities to the jungle. Among their greatest achievements was a fantastically accurate and complicated calendar that includes a precise countdown to the end of the world. On December 21, 2012, that calendar comes to an end, and a vast body of ancient Mayan prophecies announce the coming of cataclysmic change on that date.

As it happens, almost none of this is true. The ancient Mayans existed, of course, and built a brilliant and highly creative civilization in the Yucatan peninsula and the rain forests just south of it, but they didn't appear out of nowhere and they didn't vanish into thin air. Archeologists in the Mayan region can show you sites where, long before the founding of the first Mayan cities, the basic elements that later became central to Mayan culture gradually came together, and excavations elsewhere in Mexico have shown that many of the things that today's popular culture assigns to the Mayans were originally invented by older cultures— the Zapotecs of the even more ancient site of Monte Alban, for example, were using the "Mayan" calendar long before the Mayans got around to it.

As for their "disappearance," the great Mayan city-states of the southern lowlands went through a period of severe decline in the tenth century CE, involving warfare, famine, and the abandonment of most of the large urban centers, but the villagers of the countryside remained, and their descendants still live in the same area today. Elsewhere in the Mayan world, city-states on the classic model continued to flourish until the Spanish conquest of the Yucatan and Central America in the sixteenth and seventeenth centuries, and there are still plenty of people descended from the ancient Mayans, and who speak Mayan languages, throughout that part of the world.

The ancient Mayan calendar also exists, and it's a remarkable creation. It's not actually true that it keeps better time than ours according to the seasons, though. All calendars struggle to find common ground between the time taken by the Earth's rotation around its axis and the time taken by its annual journey around the Sun. Since there are 365.24219 days in a solar year, it takes some fancy mathematics to keep the calendar in step with the seasons; our calendar has been gimmicked down through the years with leap years that turn on and off depending on a list of variables, managing the trick fairly well. The Mayan calendar doesn't even try; it has no way to correct for that awkward .24219 of a day, and so its dates drift around the seasonal cycle. Its focus is elsewhere.

What really sets the Mayan calendar apart from methods of timekeeping outside of ancient Mesoamerica is the tzolkin, a cycle 260 days long, which meshes with the cycle of the year in a complex pattern that allows for very intricate timekeeping. The tzolkin is made up of two smaller cycles, a thirteen-day cycle in which each day has a number, and a twenty-day cycle in which each day has a name. Both cycles run together, so that the day 4 Ahau, for example, is followed by the day 5 Imix and the whole cycle repeats every 260 days. The tzolkin also meshes with a yearly cycle of eighteen "months" of twenty days each, plus five extra days at the end of the year; each month has a name and each day of the month has a number, so that the date 4 Ahau 3 Kankin—that is, the fourth day of the thirteen-day cycle, the last day of the twenty-day cycle, named Ahau, "Lord," and the third day of the month of Kankin, "Yellow Sun"—is a combination that only repeats once every fifty-two years.

That may seem complicated enough for anybody, but the ancient Mayans weren't finished yet. They also had another sequence, the Long Count. This was based not on the tzolkin cycle of 260 days or the natural year of 365, the haab, but on a formal year of 360 days, which was called a tun. Twenty tunob—the suffix "ob" is the Mayan plural, like "s" in English—made a katun, and twenty katunob made a baktun. The mathematics of Mayan timekeeping go well beyond the baktun; twenty baktunob make a piktun, twenty piktunob make a kalabtun, twenty kalabtunob a kinchiltun, and twenty kinchiltunob an alautun, which works out to 23,040,000,000 days, or more than sixty-three million years.

Still, even the Mayans didn't find a lot of use for counting in alautunob, and another of their important cycles followed the beat of a different numerical drum. Thirteen baktunob made up the Long Count cycle of roughly 5125 years. The current cycle began on August 13, 3114 BCE, and will end on December 21, 2012. That latter date is the one around which so many hopes and fears cluster just now.

The Mayan prophecies don't provide much raw material for these hopes and fears, for the simple reason that only one brief and not very explicit Mayan text mentions December 21, 2012 at all. Still, there's been no shortage of material from other sources to fill that gap. Pay close attention to the current crop of predictions focusing on that date—the planetary catastrophes and consciousness shifts, alien invasions and Utopian transformations being retailed to eager audiences as news of the future a little in advance—and you'll likely notice something very curious: not one of these claims is new, and in fact none of them are unique to 4 Ahau 3 Kankin 13.0.0.0.0. All of these predictions have been recycled countless times in recent years, applied to many other dates, which have nothing in common beside the fact that somebody has used them as an anchor for a prediction of the end of the world.

$$\Omega$$

These days, in fact, an astonishing number of people believe that the world as we know it is about to end suddenly, giving way to a new world to which none of today's certainties apply at all. The ones who are counting down the days to December 21, 2012, are following only one of hundreds, perhaps thousands, of belief systems that make much the same claim. Some expect the end of the world to arrive on some other date; others claim not to know the exact date but are convinced that it will happen sometime very soon.

A great many Americans, for example, are convinced that at some point in the very near future, every truly devout Protestant Christian will suddenly and mysteriously disappear from the face of the earth, going to meet Jesus in the clouds. "The Rapture," as this disappearance is called, will usher in a period of seven years, "the Tribulation," in which most of humanity will be exterminated by a succession of natural and unnatural disasters and by the minions of the world's last tyrant, "the Antichrist." At the end of the seven years, the Antichrist and all of his followers will be annihilated by Jesus, and the Christian faithful will reign with him over the world for a thousand years. Believers in this scenario are convinced that it is predicted word for word in the Christian Bible, and a very large number of them are certain that it will happen in their lifetimes.

They aren't alone in their convictions. Many devout Muslims believe in a similar version of the future; while the Rapture apparently hasn't found any echo in Muslim apocalyptic lore, the Muslim equivalent of the Antichrist, the Dajjal, is expected to be every bit as tyrannical and villainous as his Christian counterpart, and his destruction at the hands of the Mahdi, the future prophet who will lead the faithful to paradise, is as colorfully portrayed in Muslim writings as the defeat of the Antichrist by Jesus in Christian ones. Plenty of orthodox Jews, in turn, wait for the appearance of the Messiah. There are many Hindus who eagerly anticipate the birth of Kalki, the next avatar of the great god Vishnu, while Buddhists across central Asia long for the appearance of the great king Rigden Jyepo, who will ride forth from the hidden city of Shambhala to vanquish the foes of the Buddhist Dharma.

Yet the claims of religion account for only one part of the apocalyptic fervor of our times. Ask a random stranger on an American street about the end of the world and you're as likely to find yourself listening to a secular narrative as an overtly religious one. A significant number of Americans believe, for example, that aliens from a distant planet are visiting Earth secretly in flying saucers, and someday soon will make their presence known; some believe that the aliens will usher in a marvelous new age, others expect something more sinister; both groups have been waiting breathlessly for the alien presence to be disclosed to the public since the late 1940s, but both insist that disclosure is imminent and that history as we know it will soon be over.

Believers in a secular end of the world who don't find aliens to their taste have plenty of other choices. Tech-savvy intellectuals who laugh at the UFO phenomenon are as likely as not these days to believe in the Singularity, the point in the near future—one of its prophets, computer scientist Ray Kurzweil, has announced the date as 2045—when advances in artificial intelligence will lead to the creation of superintelligent computers with godlike powers who will free human beings from death and every other limitation, if they don't decide to wipe us out first. Followers of the New Age movement continue to proclaim the hope of an emerging planetary age of peace and enlightenment; on the other end of the spectrum, survivalists disappointed by the failure of the Y2K bug to plunge the world into chaos now talk about giant solar flares or asteroid collisions that could knock modern industrial society off its pedestal and give them the chance to pursue their dreams of heroic struggle in a world gone mad.

The logical conclusion is that the flurry of end-of-the-world predictions in circulation these days have little or nothing to do with the Mayan calendar's Long Count, or any of the other justifications cited for them, and a great deal more to do with something else. That "something else" is the subject of this book. Its name is *the apocalypse meme*.

Ω

What is a meme? Evolutionary biologist Richard Dawkins coined the term, in his 1976 book *The Selfish Gene*, as a label for ideas that replicate in human society the way that genes replicate in a population of living things. He extracted it from the Greek word *mimema*, "something that is imitated." Since Dawkins coined the term, the meme concept has become commonplace in the study of information, sharply criticized by some scholars and used by many others. Talk about memetics and memetic engineering, the parallels to genetics and genetic engineering, pops up now and again in avant-garde publications in a good many fields.

The core of the meme concept are the paired recognitions that ideas spread through a society in much the same way that genes spread through a population, and that natural selection works on both. A gene that produces slightly longer wings in bluebottles, for example, can survive and replicate itself in a population of bluebottles for any number of reasons: if slightly longer wings make a bluebottle more likely to survive long enough to breed, for example, or if female bluebottles find male bluebottles with longer wings more attractive, more bluebottles in each generation will have longer wings, until eventually the gene becomes all but universal in the population. The gene may provide benefits to the organism, but it doesn't have to; in fact, it may actually cause harm or death—even making the organism fall sick and die as soon as mating season is over. What makes a gene successful is simply that it improves the chances that the gene itself will be passed on.

Memes, according to meme theory, behave in the same way. A meme is an idea or a set of ideas that can be transmitted from one person to another. It survives as long as it remains a factor in somebody's thoughts and actions, and it spreads when one person convinces another to accept the meme. What makes a meme successful is simply that it encourages the people who accept it to transmit it to as many other people as possible; whether or not it has a positive impact on the lives of the people who accept it is irrelevant.

Some of the more enthusiastic meme theorists have argued that all human culture consists of memes; other researchers have challenged this on a variety of grounds. Whether or not everything humans believe and do is guided by memes, though, certain sets of ideas clearly act like memes in Dawkins's sense, replicating themselves across human communities down through the centuries, and adapting over time in much the way an organism's genetic inheritance adapts to changing conditions.

The apocalypse meme is among the most convincing examples of a meme at work. To follow it through history is to watch a distinctive set of ideas adapting and evolving over time, passing from host to host and from environment to environment, feeding on the available raw materials and fending off competing ideas with whatever defenses come to hand. Unlike many other memes, the apocalypse meme can be traced through history all the way back to its origins between 1500 and 1200 BCE, and it can be followed forward from that point right up to the present. Its trail is easy to follow for an unpleasant reason: the tracks of the apocalypse meme through history are well spattered with human blood.

Like the genes that lengthen or shorten a bluebottle's wing, again, a meme's success or failure is simply a matter of how readily it transmits from person to person. The happiness or even the survival of the individuals who accept the meme into their minds and lives are irrelevant to the meme's spread. There are some memes, to be sure, that have a consistent track record of benefiting the people who accept them, and there are many others that seem to be more or less neutral in their effects. Then there are the harmful memes—the ones that encourage people to think and act in self-defeating ways, but still manage to find new believers in every generation.

The apocalypse meme belongs to this last category. As fears and fantasies cluster thickly around 4 Ahau 3 Kankin 13.0.0.0.0, a look back over its long and disastrous history may therefore be timely.

CHAPTER ONE:

THE BEGINNING OF THE END

A strong case could be made for the idea that storytelling is one of humanity's oldest and most powerful technologies. As soon as the extraordinary gift of human language finished emerging out of whatever forgotten precursors gave it birth, hunters back from the chase and gatherers returning with nuts and tubers doubtless started describing their day's experiences in colorful terms, and their listeners picked up more than a few useful tips about how to track an antelope or wield a digging stick: the glory of the impala's leap and the comfortable fellowship of gatherers working a meadow together wove themselves into the stories and the minds of the audience, and helped shape their experience of the world. Stories still do that today, whether they're woven into the daily news, dressed up as religious or secular ideology, or in their natural form as stories one person tells another.

Some of these stories are very, very old. Most of the stories that people nowadays call "mythology," in particular, have roots that run back far into the untraceable years before anybody worked out the trick of turning spoken words into something more lasting. Read through the myths of every culture and you'll find certain themes repeated endlessly: stories of a golden age or paradise back in the distant past when things were much better than they are now; stories of a worldwide flood from which a few survivors managed to escape to repopulate the world; stories of terrible monsters and the heroes or heroines who killed them; stories of heroes or heroines of a different kind, who died so that other people might have a more abundant life—all these and others are part of the stock in trade of myth around the world, shared by peoples whose ancestors, at least until modern times, had no contact since the end of the last Ice Age.

Some modern theorists, starting from this evidence, have argued that these core themes and the stories based on them are somehow hardwired into the human brain. This may or may not be true—the jury's still out on the question—but it's definitely the case that most of the themes of mythology appear on every continent and in every age. If they were invented, the event happened so long ago that no trace remains of the inventor or the time and circumstances of the invention.

The apocalypse meme is one of the few exceptions. Hard work by a handful of perceptive scholars, most notably historian of religions Norman Cohn, has traced it back to a specific place, time, and person. The place was the rugged region of south central Asia that today is called Iran, the time was somewhere between 1500 and 1200 BCE, and the person was Zarathustra, the prophet of the religion now called Zoroastrianism.

Ω

Very little is known for sure about Zarathustra. Until recently, even the time when he lived was open to question; a traditional date among today's Zoroastrians claimed that their founder's career took place in the middle of the sixth century BCE, while internal evidence in the oldest parts of the Avesta, the Zoroastrian scriptures, pointed to a date at least six centuries further back. Only in recent decades has the evidence for the older date become conclusive and allowed the evidence of archeology to cast a little more light on the enigmatic figure of the world's first prophet of apocalypse.

Iran in those days was a land of small villages whose inhabitants survived mostly on the yields of their herds and flocks. They worshipped a pantheon of gods not too different from those of their neighbors, with a thunder god who brought the annual rains and an assortment of other deities associated with the forces of nature. Like most of their neighbors, too, they had a caste of priests who recited

3

the traditional stories about the gods from memory, and officiated at sacrifices. Zarathustra was raised and educated to be one of these priests.

Exactly what the young Zarathustra studied in his apprenticeship is a question that has attracted a surprising amount of attention over the last century and a half or so. Partly that attention came from the fact that the archaic Persian dialect in which the oldest Zoroastrian scriptures are written is among the very oldest languages in the Indo-European language family, to which most of the languages of Europe belong, and thus appealed to nineteenth-century European scholars interested in the origins of their own cultures; partly it comes from the fact that the Zoroastrian religion is the oldest surviving monotheistic religion on Earth, and thus caught the attention, again, of nineteenth-century European scholars, most of whom belonged to a later and much more widespread monotheist faith. Beyond these specific interests, though, lay an immense and now mostly forgotten attempt carried out by hundreds of scholars in the nineteenth and early twentieth centuries to find some single key to the world's mythologies.

Until the end of the eighteenth century, most of the scholars who tried to figure out the meanings of the world's myths drew from a very limited stock of possible answers. One theory, always very popular, insisted that whatever myths the scholar's own people happened to believe were truth, pure and simple, and every other mythology was either simple ignorance or a pack of lies spread by some evil spirit or other. Another theory noted the deep similarities among myths, and imagined some original set of religious teachings long ago that had been reworked and distorted over time into the myths known to history. Still another theory, first suggested in ancient Greece by a man named Euhemerus, and named "euhemerism" after him, held that the events of myth were dim memories of historical events in the distant past, stretched out of shape by storytellers over the generations.

Beginning in the nineteenth century, though, many of the scholars that studied myth began to pay attention to the hints and traces woven into mythologies from around the world, which suggested that an important set of meanings for myth could be found in the heavens. Their work fell out of academic fashion in the middle years of the twentieth century and remains largely in eclipse today, but merits a serious reappraisal; though their identification of mythology and astronomy was too often stretched to include all myth everywhere—a bad habit shared with almost every other interpretation of mythology—the recognition that at least some myth has a strong astronomical dimension rests on too much evidence to be casually dismissed.

Most people know that the gods and goddesses of ancient religions from around the world were very often associated with the Sun, the Moon, the visible planets, and the constellations—for that matter, we still call the planets by the names of old gods—but the connections go much further and deeper than that. Consider the story of the warrior-child Kullervo from the Kalevala, the great myth-cycle of Finland. At one point in his many adventures, Kullervo is thrown into the ocean by his wicked uncle, who hopes to drown him, but the child is found later measuring the entire ocean in a ladle; it comes to a little over two ladles full. Who is it that measures the Great Deep in a little over two measures? The warrior-planet Mars, of course, with its orbital period of 2.2 of Earth's years.

There are thousands of such examples running all through the world's mythologies that suddenly make sense when interpreted by way of the facts of astronomy. Why, though, would people make up colorful stories to describe the movements of the planets and the cycle of the seasons? From our modern standpoint, surrounded as we are by books and calendars, this seems like an absurd way of doing things, but it makes perfect sense when placed in the context of a time before writing, when the only way to preserve important knowledge for the future was to make sure that it could be remembered.

Myths are memorable. It takes much less effort to learn a story like that of Kullervo by heart than it takes to memorize a table of dry facts about the movements of the planet Mars, and if the story is put into verse—and most ancient myths were—the rhythm and poetry of the language becomes a powerful help to the memory. Even in today's world, when memory is by and large neglected, most people can instantly remember the nursery rhymes they learned in childhood and the lyrics to the popular songs of their teen years. Put the same power of memory to work on wild, colorful narratives that encode valuable knowledge, and it's easy to see how mythology could become a potent tool for information storage and transfer at a time when writing had not yet been imagined.

Many different kinds of knowledge must have been turned into mythic stories and committed to memory in ancient times, just as many different kinds of knowledge are preserved in stories and poetry among nonliterate societies today. Still, among the many cultures that took to agriculture, growing their own food rather than relying on nature to produce it for them, astronomy would have been a crucial body of knowledge. In an age before written calendars and almanacs, how did farmers know when it was time to plant their crops and carry out all the other seasonally dependent chores of the agricultural year? There were plenty of cues that could be read from nature—to this day, for example, farmers and gardeners in the Appalachian Mountains will tell you that it's time to plant corn when the leaves on the oak trees are the size of a mouse's ear—but above and behind them all stood the turning heavens, a clock and calendar for those who knew how to read them.

Know exactly where on the horizon the Sun rises on the day of the spring equinox, in particular, and you have a precise measure for the arrival of spring. Know what stars rise in the gray dawn before sunrise or the dusk after sunset during every season and you have a measure of time you can apply at any time of the year. Know the longer cycles—Mars, which takes 2.2 years to circle through the heavens; Jupiter, which takes twelve years; Saturn, which takes nearly thirty—and you have a tool that can master time and track the generations.

Most of these measures of time rely on tracking the Sun, the Moon, and the visible planets as they move relative to the backdrop of the stars. Keep following those movements for long enough, though, and you will discover something unsettling: the backdrop of the stars also seems to move. Over the generations, this movement causes drastic displacements in the heavens. The pole star of one century moves gradually away from the pole, and is replaced by another that used to be farther away. The stars that used to rise just before the Sun on the spring equinox no longer do so, and other stars must be chosen. This slow shift of the starry heavens thus became one of the core teachings of the old mythic starlore, and became deeply woven into the worldviews and religious concepts of ancient peoples around the world.

Ω

The shift in question is called the precession of the equinoxes. It's caused by a slow wobble in the axis around which the Earth rotates—a very slow wobble, as it takes more than twenty-five thousand years to complete a full circle. Over that period, the wobble makes the position of the Sun relative to the background of stars at the solstices and equinoxes seem to slip backwards through the zodiac, the circle of constellations that marks out the Sun's apparent track across the heavens, at a rate of around one degree every seventy-two years.

At present, the Sun at the time of the spring equinox appears from Earth to be located in front of an area of faint stars between the constellations Pisces and Aquarius. A little over two thousand years ago it was moving into Pisces out of Aries; two thousand years before that, it was leaving Taurus behind and moving into Aries, while two thousand years from now it will be most of the way through Aquarius, heading toward Capricorn. Since the cycle of precession is caused by a wobble in Earth's rotation, none of these details apply anywhere else in the universe; on the off chance that our descendants colonize Mars, they will have to work it out for themselves, since the axis around which Mars rotates is at a different angle from Earth's and most likely wobbles at a different rate.

According to most modern historians of science, nobody accomplished that same task here on Earth until the second century BCE, when the Greek astronomer Hipparchus noted that the stars had shifted from the positions assigned to them in old records. Within a few centuries after Hipparchus's time, the precession had been analyzed precisely enough that Greek and Roman scientists had a specific figure for the Great Year, the period over which the Sun's location at the spring equinox circles all the way around the zodiac: 25,920 years, which they divided into twelve Great Months of 2,160 years each. It was in this form that precession became a theme in Western culture, with echoes right up to the present. Those old enough to remember the days when the dawning of the Age of Aquarius was a hot cultural theme know at least one of those echoes: the Age of Aquarius is the Great Month in which the Sun's position at the spring equinox is in the constellation Aquarius.

On the other side of the Atlantic from Hipparchus and his followers, and probably a few centuries later, the ancient Mayans—or possibly one of the earlier Mesoamerican cultures that gave the Mayans their calendar and some of their mathematics—also noticed the phenomenon of precession. Their estimate for the Great Year was a little different: 25,625 years, which they divided into five subdivisions rather than twelve. Each one of those subdivisions was a Long Count cycle of thirteen baktunob, or 5125 years, and it's one of these cycles that is coming to an end on December 21, 2012.

Still, there are good reasons to think that other people who watched the skies caught the slow rhythm of the precession of the equinoxes many centuries before the Greeks or the Mayans. One of those reasons is that the ancients had a very efficient method of double-checking the seasons, one that would have forced them to notice precession within a few generations.

One of the best places to observe the double-checking process is also the most famous prehistoric structure anywhere on Earth: Stonehenge. On the morning of the summer solstice, as you stand in the center of Stonehenge and look northeast past the Heel Stone, the Sun rises over a specific point on the eastern horizon, and seems to brush the Heel Stone as it climbs into the sky. There are similar though less spectacular markers for midsummer sunset and for the sunrises and sunsets at other important points in the year's cycle. Those points don't change with the precession of the equinoxes, so the ancient priests or priestesses who tracked the seasons from Stonehenge when it was new would have discovered easily enough that the stars that rose just before the Sun, or set just after it, on the solstices and equinoxes changed over time.

The other crucial reason to think that ancient peoples knew about precession long before Hipparchus's time is that the old mythological lore is riddled with references to it. Historians of science Giorgio de Santillana and Hertha von Dechend filled a very large book, *Hamlet's Mill: An Essay on Myth and the Frame of Time*, with examples from the world's mythologies, and even so they themselves admitted that they had barely scratched the surface of an extraordinarily rich body of archaic starlore, much of it centered on precession.

Across much of the world, the myths that teach about precession have a distinctive form. The oldest expressions of that form describe a series of great ages of the world, each of them governed by its own ruling powers, who are destined to be displaced and overthrown by the powers of the age that follows in a titanic struggle that shatters the entire cosmos. In a sense, this is exactly what happens at the end of a precessional age, because the framework of the cosmos— the stars that indicate "the four corners of the world," or in modern language, the Sun's position at the solstices and equinoxes—goes out of whack and has to be replaced.

In many of the old traditions, the rulers of the cosmos in each of the precessional ages were identified as gods and goddesses. This seems odd to people nowadays, not least because it meant that certain gods and goddesses died or were displaced from their celestial thrones, and we don't

11

tend to think of death as an occupational hazard of divinity any more. Still, the polytheist religions of the past had very different attitudes toward the divine. In the ancient Greek world of Hipparchus's time, people on the island of Crete revered a shrine on Mount Jouktas where Zeus, the king of the gods, was buried; in today's Japan, followers of the Shinto faith consider the great shrine at Tsubaki, in Mie Prefecture, to be located on the site of the grave of the Shinto earth deity Sarutahiko-no-Ōkami. Neither the ancient Greeks nor the modern Japanese consider the fact that the deities in question died and were buried to be any impediment to their ability to function as gods, and of course a god who died but is still believed to be around to answer prayers is central to the most popular religion of the Western world as well.

In a great many of the more recent versions of the precessional myth, however, the rulers of each age of the world were no longer seen as gods; instead, they came to be identified with legendary kings and queens, the ages of the world themselves were turned into kingdoms, and the overturning of the world at the end of an age was retold as a great war between the kingdoms in which the old order perished and a new dynasty rose to power. Look closely at the kings and their struggles for power and peace, though, and it's not hard to recognize that they represent stars—the heavenly markers of the seasons, shifting slowly relative to the Sun's position at the solstices and equinoxes, dressed up in colorful names and heroic adventures to make them memorable in an age before writing.

In Iran, more than two thousand years after Zarathustra's time, just such a cycle of legends became the subject of one of the world's great epics: the *Shah-nameh* or Book of Kings, composed by the Persian poet Firdausi around the year 1010 CE. There the two world-orders have become the kingdoms of Turan and Iran, the former ruled by the villainous king Afrasiab and the latter by the heroic prince Kai Khusrau. The struggle between them ends with Kai Khusrau's triumph, and he takes the title "Lord of Aries." Why Aries? Because this was the constellation in which the Sun appeared at the spring equinox once Kai Khusrau or, more precisely, the star he represented, became the marker of the spring equinox.

None of this was new in Firdausi's time. The Gathas, a collection of poems that are the oldest of the Zoroastrian scriptures—some of them may in fact have been written by Zarathustra himself—mention figures who later on became characters in the Shah-nameh, Kai Khusrau and Afrasiab among them. Further back, pieced together in the nineteenth century by industrious scholars, lay the vast body of archaic starlore embodied in these later tales, the ancient myths that enabled the priests of ancient Iran to track the cycles of the seasons and reminded them that the ruling stars that provided them with their calendar would someday fall from their thrones and be replaced by others.

Ω

This was the lore, in other words, that Zarathustra studied as an apprentice priest. Around the time he turned twenty, however, Zarathustra experienced a shattering vision in which Ahura Mazda, "Lord Wisdom," the only true god, appeared to him surrounded by six subordinate spirits, the Amesha Spentas or "Holy Immortals." In place of the symbolic struggle between world orders that shaped the starlore he had learned, the vision revealed to him a new and far more intense moral struggle, for against the power of Ahura Mazda and his Holy Immortals were ranged Angra Mainyu, the spirit of the Lie, and a host of demons who were mostly borrowed from the older Iranian gods. That struggle was not limited to the time when one set of stars gave way to another as markers of the seasons; it began, Zarathustra came to believe, with the beginning of the world, but it would come to an end sometime in the not too distant future with the final defeat of Angra Mainyu and the power of the Lie.

With the coming of the Zorostrian apocalypse, the Frashegird—literally, "the making wonderful"—all sorrow, suffering, illness, and death would end forever, the dead would come back to life, and faithful believers in Zarathustra's teachings would enter into an eternity of bliss, while those who rejected the true faith would be forced to wade through torrents of molten metal and the like. Ahura Mazda's instrument in bringing about this great change was the Saoshyant, a messianic figure born of the seed of Zarathustra, who would take up the sword and lead the legions of the faithful against the powers of Lie and vanquish them forever.

This sort of thinking seems very familiar to most people nowadays, and for good reason; such rhetoric appears in endlessly repeated forms in most modern religions. What makes this repetition fascinating is that in Zarathustra's time nearly all of these ideas were brand new. The polytheist faith in which Zarathustra himself was raised, like polytheist faiths around the world, had no place for them because they had no need of them. Zarathustra was apparently one of the world's first monotheists, and it is a testament to his intellectual powers and essential honesty that he faced the core contradiction of monotheism squarely, and proposed what has been the standard response to that contradiction ever since.

The contradiction is usually called the problem of evil. It can be stated very simply: if there is one and only one god, and that god is infinitely powerful, wise, and loving, why is there so much misery in the world? Polytheist faiths don't trouble much with this question because polytheism offers built-in answers to it. To begin with, the gods and goddesses of polytheist faiths are mighty, but they're not almighty, and there are corresponding limits to their wisdom and beneficence; thus there can be evils in the world that not even a god is powerful enough, clever enough, or motivated enough to overcome. Furthermore, the gods and goddesses of polytheist faiths routinely quarrel with one another, and so it's always possible for the good done by one deity to be undone by the actions of another. Thus it's never hard for polytheists to figure out why suffering happens; when it does happen, they can always try to figure out what god or goddess was offended, and make offerings in the hope of getting the deity into a better mood, and if that doesn't work, they can console themselves with the reflection that sometimes even the gods have bad days.

Monotheist faiths have none of these advantages. A god who is all-powerful and all-knowing would by definition have the means and opportunity to get rid of all evil and suffering, and a god who is all-loving would have the motive. Theologians and philosophers since the early days of monotheism have therefore had to put in long hours coming up with reasons why evil and suffering so often happen anyway. Any number of theories have been proposed down through the millennia, but nearly all of them rely on the proposal Zarathustra offered right at the dawn of monotheism itself: that the world in which evil and suffering exist is a temporary, ramshackle structure, and will sometime very soon be replaced by an eternal, perfect world in which evil and suffering will have vanished forever.

Behind this vision of a final conflict between good and evil, ending in the permanent elimination of evil, the mythological forms of the ancient starlore are easy to spot. The struggle between Kai Khusrau and Afrasiab, though, was not a conflict between absolute good and absolute evil; for all his villainies, Afrasiab had his virtues, and many of the warriors who fought on his side of the great struggle were just as noble and chivalrous as the paladins who served

Kai Khusrau. Equally, the victory of Kai Khusrau was never expected to be permanent, and the *Shah-nameh* goes on to record plenty of battles, derring-do, and evil deeds by villainous figures in the reigns of his successors. Understood as a way of talking about precession, all this makes perfect sense, since the great wheel of the heavens did not stop turning when Kai Khusrau's star moved into its temporary position as the marker of spring.

This, of course, marks the core of the transformation Zarathustra carried out on the archaic precessional myths. From myths of the temporary victory of a figure representing cosmic order meant to be understood at least partly in metaphoric terms, he crafted a new myth of the absolute and permanent victory of a figure representing cosmic order meant to be understood in an absolutely literal fashion. The triumph of the Saoshyant and the legions of Ahura Mazda over Angra Mainyu and the demons of the Lie, in turn, wasn't simply expected to straighten out the calendar and put the seasons in order; it was meant to straighten out everything and put the entire world into order, or more specifically, the order Zarathustra thought it should have—one in which, inevitably, those people who disagreed with him were going to have a very rough time of it.

Zarathustra's fellow priests don't seem to have thought much of all this. According to tradition, which in this case seems reasonable enough, Zarathustra suffered persecution and poverty as a result of his newfound faith. After years of wandering, however, he found support at the court of Vishtaspa, the king—we would probably use the label "chieftain" for such a figure nowadays—of a tribe in eastern Iran. There Zarathustra found his first converts, including the king; there he married a woman from a wealthy family; there he taught his followers; and when the priests of the older religion incited neighboring chieftains to go to war against the upstart faith, it was from Vishtaspa's court that Zarathustra preached the world's first holy war, and bought the survival of his teachings with the blood of its enemies.

According to some accounts, Zarathustra himself was killed in the fighting. If this is what happened, the creator of the apocalypse meme was also its first martyr. There is a certain ironic appropriateness to this, for the meme's first martyr would not be its last.

Ω

In the centuries that followed Zarathustra's lifetime, his faith spread through much of southern Asia and sent missionaries—another Zoroastrian innovation—out in all directions. In the sixth century BCE, it became the state religion of the Persian Empire, the largest empire the world had seen up to that time, and the patronage of an imperial government boosted Zoroastrianism to its all-time peak.

Missionary zeal combined with the prestige of a superpower seeded Zarathustra's ideas across much of Eurasia, though not all those seeds grew into replicas of the parent plant. In the country along the banks of the river Don that would later become the historic core of Russia, for example, kings and peasants alike listened to the missionaries but could not be talked into putting aside their traditional worship of the thunder god Perun and the lively pantheon over which he presided; they simply made room for two more gods, Chernobog the Black God and Byelobog the White God, whose unending struggle for supremacy gave storytellers another theme to keep their audiences entranced on long winter nights.

Far to the east, in China, Zarathustra's ideas had more serious consequences. There the concepts of yang and yin— originally words meaning "the sunny side of a hill" and "the shady side of a hill," but gradually expanding to embrace every opposition in the world of human experience—had become basic categories of thought. These concepts gave rise to the *I Ching* or Book of Changes, which remains to this day the most elegant and comprehensive expression of the archaic vision of cyclic change and renewal, and they played a major role in shaping the philosophy of Taoism. During the earliest centuries of Chinese civilization, China was racked with wars and social unrest, and it had plenty of visionary thinkers who claimed to be able to offer better ways to handle the crises of their time; still, none of them taught that the universe would hand them a perfect world in the near future.

That claim was left to a slightly later age. Just when Zoroastrian ideas got to China and brought the apocalypse meme with them is still an open question, but get there they did; by the year 142 CE, certainly, they were well enough naturalized to launch a religious movement on Chinese soil. It was in this year that Chang Taoling, a Taoist mystic living in a cave in Szechwan province, had a vision remarkably like Zarathustra's. In that vision Lao Tzu, the traditional founder of Taoism, appeared in glory to tell Chang Taoling that all the gods then worshipped by the Chinese people were "dead energies," that the six heavens of the false gods had perished and the three heavens of the true Taoist faith now ruled the cosmos, and that the idyllic Heavenly Kingdom of Great Peace would shortly become manifested on Earth.

Chang's vision became the mainspring of a popular religious movement, and attracted plenty of interest outside its membership. It did not take long, as a result, before the vision of a perfect world about to arrive combined with a time of troubles in the Chinese Empire to provide an opening that a handful of ambitious men were ready, willing, and able to exploit.

Shang Jue and his two younger brothers, Shang Liang and Shang Pao, were the men in question. Like many other apocalyptic thinkers before and since, they seem to have combined a passionate faith in the prophecies of their religion with an equally intense craving for political power. The religious sect they led, the Way of Great Peace, taught that the world was about to end in a vast catastrophe; that Lao Tzu would miraculously return to Earth in order to protect the faithful members of the sect during the cataclysm; and that as a mark of the great change about to happen, the sky would change from blue to the sacred color yellow. "The Blue Heaven will pass away, the Yellow Heaven will arise" was the Yellow Turban slogan, and the yellow cloths they tied around their heads—the source of their movement's common name—represented the coming yellow sky.

All this happened late in the second century CE, in the years just before 184. That was a promising time for such ventures. The emperor on the throne, Han Ling, was a weak man who allowed the court eunuchs to manage the empire's affairs, which they did in a style unusually corrupt even by the standards of the time. Their mismanagement allowed wealthy landowners to exploit the rural poor, and the plight of the latter was made worse by high taxes and floods along the Yellow River valley. Desperate people make good recruits for apocalyptic cults and revolutionary parties. Shang Jue's movement was more than a little bit of both, and it attracted many adherents from every part of China.

As the Yellow Turban movement grew, Shang Jue laid plans for a mass insurgency in the spring of 184, starting with a sudden assault on the imperial palace. His plans were betrayed to the government, however, and he had to flee the capital at Loyang for the northern provinces in the middle of winter. As soon as he had reached safe territory, he raised the banner of revolt. Caught half prepared, the imperial forces lost several early battles, but by the summer of 184 the tide had turned in the government's favor, and by the end of that year all three of the Shang brothers and most of their followers were dead. Sporadic Yellow Turban risings continued for several years thereafter, but never again managed to pose a significant threat to the imperial government, and these risings generally ended with mass executions of everyone who had been involved in them.

Most other memes would probably have died out promptly in the face of total failure and the savage repression that followed, but the apocalypse meme has a curious feature: it thrives on humiliation and defeat. As the empire came unglued in the decades following the Yellow Turban rising—the Han Dynasty collapsed in 220 CE, and was followed by a long age in which warring kingdoms struggled for supremacy—underground movements copying the Yellow Turban model began to surface, and they kept on surfacing for decades, centuries, and millennia, like a series of broken records replaying the Yellow Turbans' song of conspiracy, rebellion, and failure.

The movement set in motion by Chang Taoling, curiously enough, managed to become one of the few exceptions. Sometime after the Han Dynasty collapsed, Chang's successors—the Heavenly Masters, who established a permanent base at a Taoist monastery on Dragon-Tiger Mountain in north China—seem to have decided that the Heavenly Kingdom of Great Peace was going to have to be a spiritual state rather than a political reality, and acted accordingly. The profound pragmatism of the Taoist tradition managed, in this one case, to overcome the lure of the apocalypse meme and launch the sect of the Heavenly Masters onto a very different trajectory. Almost two thousand years later, there is still a Heavenly Master, though the sect has been headquartered on Taiwan since the Communist revolution of 1949, and Taoist priests still seek ordination from the current Heavenly Master as proof of their right to practice the mysteries of the Tao.

Other inheritors of the meme have not been so fortunate. Every one of the dynasties that ruled China after the Han, right up to the day the Manchu Dynasty fell in 1911, had to deal with actual or threatened rebellions on the part of underground sects who were convinced that the Mandate of Heaven had passed to them and the existing dynasty would be overthrown by supernatural forces. As new religious traditions reached China—Buddhism a few centuries after the Han Dynasty ended, for example, and Christianity a few centuries later—the tradition of Chinese apocalyptic rebellion absorbed useful ideas from these sources but kept its basic character intact. This form of the apocalypse meme never failed to find new takers, even though none of these revolts succeeded in its aims, and nearly all of them ended with the mass extermination of their followers at the hands of imperial troops.

Today, almost two thousand years after the Yellow Turban revolt, sects along the same lines can still be found in Taiwan and Chinese expatriate communities around the world, though it has been a while since any of them have tried to usher in a new age of the world by force; the lessons taught by two thousand years of total failure may finally have been learned. It's anyone's guess whether sects of the same kind still exist in the People's Republic of China. Still, the harsh treatment dealt out by the Chinese government to the Falun Dafa sect a few years ago shows clearly enough that in Beijing, at least, the Yellow Turbans have not been forgotten.

As one of the centers of world culture, not to mention

one of the planet's superpowers for most of the last three thousand years, China might have seemed a likely springboard from which the apocalypse meme could have launched itself around the world. Oddly, though, this isn't what happened. The distinctive Chinese version of the meme has managed to drive some two thousand years of failed Utopian dreams and futile violence within China, but it has shown little ability to spread beyond Chinese territory. Even those nations most powerfully influenced by China's example down through the centuries—Japan, Korea, Vietnam, Tibet—have drawn on other sources for their visions of imminent doom.

The irony, and it's a rich one, is that the nation that played the role that China didn't—the springboard by which the apocalypse meme leapt from its Persian origins to its present pandemic status—was a tiny Middle Eastern kingdom that only existed for a few centuries, and during that time, was of no particular importance to anyone more than a few miles outside its borders. Adding to the irony is the fact that the kingdom didn't begin to fulfill its role as a carrier of the meme until well after it ceased to exist, and its people began the first stage of an exile that would end by scattering them around the world. The kingdom, of course, was the nation of Judah, and its people are the Jews.

CHAPTER TWO:

THE CRUCIBLE OF JUDAISM

For nearly two thousand years now, across an area that originally extended from Ireland to India and now embraces the globe, cultural forces driven by the teachings of two great missionary religions—Islam and Christianity—have conspired to make the ancient kingdom of Judah and its northern neighbor Israel look far more important than they actually were. The oral traditions, folktales, and poetry that were assembled in the sixth century BCE into the Jewish scriptures provided Christianity with its Old Testament and Islam with many of its central concepts and narratives, and since both these religions insist on their own universal relevance, the doings of the kings, prophets, and peoples of these two otherwise unimportant nations have been redefined on the same grand scale.

The mismatch between the sweeping importance credited to the ancient Jewish kingdoms retrospectively, through the eyes of faith, and their actual importance in the context of their own time and place can be measured by the simple fact that the entire kingdom of Judah, at its greatest extent, was all of twenty-five miles across. The northern kingdom of Israel was a little larger, and during the two kingdoms' brief period of unity—which lasted almost exactly a century, during the reigns of the three kings Saul, David, and Solomon—it received tribute from, and exercised some degree of power over, half a dozen little kingdoms on the same scale surrounding it. There were quite literally hundreds of other kingdoms in the same broad region that had similar histories and achieved, at one or another point in their histories, the same sort of micro-empire over their neighbors.

All the efforts of archeologists and historians have failed to come up with much in the way of significant differences between the little city-state of Judah and the hundreds of other tiny kingdoms that made up so much of the political fabric of the ancient world. Like its neighbors, or for that matter its close equivalents for anything up to a thousand miles in any direction you care to look, Judah was in theory a hereditary monarchy; in practice, a capable and canny war leader from a poor family could get himself onto the throne, as David did after the death of Saul. Judah's economy was rooted in the timeless rhythms of subsistence agriculture and animal herding, carried out by a peasant class who made up the vast majority of the population, and who supported by their labor a small minority of craftsmen, soldiers, priests, and aristocrats. It had a city at its center, though this would barely count as a small town by modern standards—Jerusalem, the political and religious metropolis of Judah, covered maybe a quarter of a square mile during the reign of King Solomon.

At the center of each of these little kingdoms was the national temple. Judah's temple, the Temple of Solomon, has been the focus of some of the world's most overblown rhetoric, but it was simply another example of the type. Like its equivalents elsewhere in the ancient world, it was an attractive building, made of stone and Lebanese cedar and ornamented with plenty of gold, but by modern standards it was a bit on the small side; according to 1 Kings 6, which gives the measurements, it was all of one hundred feet long, thirty-three feet wide, and fifty feet high.

The temple, in turn, was the focus of the national religion, and here again the differences between that religion and those of its neighbors were much less significant than the rhetoric of later ages has made it appear. Every little kingdom in the ancient world had its national god, in much the same way that the kingdoms of medieval Europe each had its patron saint. From Enlil, the national god of the Sumerian city of Nippur, to Athena, the national goddess of the Greek city of Athens, these deities, their powers, and their relationships to their worshippers differed surprisingly little.

Each little kingdom had a covenant with its guardian deity, who undertook to defend it from its enemies, ward off whatever troubles might come its way, bring the seasons and their harvests in due time, and provide the kingdom's leaders with guidance by way of some sort of traditional oracle or divination—the Urim and Thummim in the Temple of Solomon, and the ecstatic trances of the ancient Jewish prophets, are classic examples of the kind—in exchange for regular offerings at the national temple and the precise maintenance of some not too demanding set of taboos. One of those taboos marked one of the very few noticeable differences between the god of Judah and those of its neighbors: unlike most deities of the time, the god in the temple of Jerusalem was not represented by a statue, and indeed making any images of him was banned by traditional laws.

None of the ancient faiths, interestingly enough, ever seem to have claimed that their national god was the only god that existed, or even the only god that mattered. Monotheism was not quite unknown during the age when Judea's temple flourished; the Zoroastrians in distant Persia were doubtless a subject of travelers' tales, and there had been one brief but dramatic outburst closer to home in Egypt. In the middle years of the fourteenth century BCE, the heretic pharaoh Akhenaten had attempted to abolish Egypt's traditional religion—a patchwork of standard-issue city-state cults stitched together into a loose and comfortable pantheon—in favor of the worship of the one god Aten, with himself as Aten's priest and prophet. Akhenaten's seventeen-year reign had been a total disaster for Egypt, and his successors tipped every trace of his religious revolution into history's dumpster as quickly as they could after his death. There may have been folk memories of his time circulating in the Middle East four centuries later, when the Temple of Solomon was built, but there's precisely no evidence that anybody in Judah paid the least attention to them.

The oldest strata of the Jewish scriptures bear witness to this state of affairs. In ways that have been an embarrassment to strict monotheists ever since, passages in the Old Testament assume that the national god of Judah was simply that, without any trace of the far more exalted status his worshippers claimed for him in the centuries to come. Consider the comment of Jephthah, one of the judges of the Hebrews in the years before the foundation of the monarchy at Jerusalem, to the king of Ammon, another small kingdom of the time: "Wilt thou not possess that which Chemosh thy god giveth thee to possess? So whomsoever the Lord our God shall drive out from before us, them will we possess" (Judges 11:24). For that matter, the first commandment—"Thou shalt have no other gods before me"—presupposes that there are other gods, and simply requires that the Hebrews put their own national god first.

Nor does it ever seem to have occurred to the worshippers of Yahweh, the god of Judah and Israel, that someday soon their god could be expected to exterminate much of the human race, turn the established order of nature on its head, and bring on a new and everlasting age in which a Jewish monarch would rule the world and every nation would be subject to the Jews. The most anybody in the ancient world asked from their gods was victory in war, prosperity in peace, good health and good fortune for individuals, and maybe the occasional glimpse into a future that was assumed to be pretty much like the present. For the people of that time, those blessings seemed entirely adequate.

In the days when Judah was still an independent kingdom, in other words, the apocalypse meme had not yet spread west from Iran. When it did so, in the wake of political and military catastrophe, it set shock waves in motion that have not yet faded out.

Ω

One of the worst things that can happen to a small nation is to find itself sandwiched between two big nations. Belgium comes to mind; it's been one of the world's most inoffensive nations for most of its history, but because it borders France on one side and Germany on the other, it normally gets the stuffing pounded out of it whenever war breaks out in western Europe. There are plenty of other examples, but the extreme case is the narrow strip of land between the eastern shore of the Mediterranean and the valley of the Jordan River, where the little kingdom of Judah and its neighbors farmed and fought and worshipped their national gods.

Most of the military history of the ancient Mediterranean world ebbed and flowed along that corridor between the sea and the Judean hills. The stage on which Judah had its brief interval of existence was set by one such tide of war. Around 1300 BCE, a flood tide of barbarian invaders—the

Peoples of the Sea—surged south from somewhere north of Greece, overwhelmed the mighty Hittite Empire in what is now Turkey, sacked and burned the ancient city-states of the coastal plains, and finally went down in defeat in two titanic battles against the massed armies and fleets of Egypt. The aftermath saw Egypt and the grim militaristic kingdom of Assyria, in what is now northern Iraq, become the super-powers of the age.

Judah's emergence and history as an independent kingdom took place entirely under the shadow of the resulting balance of power. It's entirely possible that the tribes of the Judean hill country were originally descended from refugees from Egypt, as the Book of Exodus claims, and the Book of Judges presents a very plausible image of Jewish history between the arrival of the refugees in the hill country and the emergence of the monarchy under Saul: the story of a loose alliance of hill tribes, impoverished even by the standards of the time, who managed to unite under a series of chieftains to defend themselves against neigh-boring peoples. Over a period of several centuries, they first fought off attempts at conquest by the Philistines—a more civilized people whose cities lay along the Mediterranean coast—then turned the tables and gradually made good their claim to the coastal plains, with their lucrative trade routes and seaports.

Around 1000 BCE, while both Egypt and Assyria were preoccupied with crises elsewhere, the warrior kings Saul and David turned the alliance of tribes into a unified state with its capital at Jerusalem. That period of relative isolation closed not long after the death of Solomon and the division of his kingdom, though, and thereafter Judah and its northern neighbor Israel had to contend not only with local city-states but also with the greatest empires of the age. In the late eighth century BCE, as a result, as the balance of power swung their way, the Assyrians conquered Israel and deported its upper classes to the far corners of the Assyrian Empire.

Judah survived as a vassal kingdom for another century, and still had its own monarchy when the Assyrian Empire suddenly collapsed at the end of the seventh century. The Babylonian Empire, which replaced Assyria, had less tolerant policies than its predecessor, and in 597 BCE, the king and most of the upper classes of Judea were deported as hostages to Babylon. A few years later, the new king of Judea, Zedekiah, tried to regain his nation's independence by allying with Egypt, and the Babylonian response was drastic. In 586 BCE, Jerusalem was sacked and burned, the temple was demolished, the last king had his eyes burnt out with hot irons and was led away in chains to Babylon, and a much larger section of Judea's population was deported along with him to share the fate of the earlier hostages.

There the story of the Jews might well have ended. The Jewish exiles in Babylon spent their time fretting about the past and spinning wild dreams about a future when they would return triumphantly to their homeland, yet the same things have been done by many other émigré communities down through the centuries, usually with little result. Still, the story of Judea didn't have the usual ending, because in the case of the Jews, it turned out that some of those wild dreams were destined to come true.

Mighty as it seemed from the standpoint of little Judah, the Babylonian Empire was a brittle, ramshackle mess that had been tacked together in a hurry to fill the political vacuum left by the Assyrian collapse. Most of its territory was occupied by sullen subject peoples, who felt no loyalty to their new overlords, a fact that goes far to explain the harsh measures dealt out in response to Judah's attempt at rebellion. Egypt remained a threat on its western borders, while a far more dangerous enemy—the rising power of Persia—was taking shape in the highlands off to the east. It was the latter that eventually doomed Babylon; less than half a century after the destruction of Jerusalem, in 538 BCE, Persian armies surged out of Iran, broke through the Babylonian frontier defenses, fought their way across the Euphrates plain to the city of Babylon itself and conquered it. This decapitation strike ended Babylon's Empire very nearly overnight, and by the time the dust finally settled, the Persian Empire extended straight across the Middle East from eastern Iran to the shores of the Mediterranean.

The Persian conquest opened up a window of opportunity that the Jewish exile community moved quickly to exploit. Cyrus, the Persian emperor, was a canny politician as well as a brilliant general, and he set out to win the loyalty of the peoples he had conquered by abolishing the most detested and burdensome of the Babylonian Empire's policies. Judah itself was simply another Persian province by then, and so it cost Cyrus nothing at all to permit the Jewish exiles in Babylon to head back to their homeland and begin to rebuild. The move gained him, in a corner of his empire that was exposed to foreign intrigues, a provincial government and upper class that owed everything to Persia. That's how things worked out, too: for the next three centuries, until the Persian Empire was destroyed in its turn by the Greek armies of Alexander the Great, Judah was one of the few corners of the Persian Empire where Cyrus's heirs never had to worry about rebellion.

The decision to let a group of Jewish exiles return to Jerusalem and rebuild their city and temple turned out, though, to have even more sweeping consequences for the future. The national religion of the exiles that returned from Babylon was no longer the temple cult of a local deity of the sort that could be found from one end to the other of the Mediterranean world. The deity whose deeds were proclaimed in those scriptures had suddenly changed from the god of a little kingdom into the one true god of the entire cosmos, the creator of the world and everything in it. The folktales and poems that the exiles recalled from their people's tribal past, in turn, were gathered up, written down, and thoroughly edited to fit this new set of concepts, and the process created the Jewish scriptures more or less as they exist today.

What had happened is clear enough. The returning exiles had reshaped their traditional religious beliefs in the image of the Zoroastrian faith of their Persian overlords. This sort of thing is common enough in the history of religions. Even the most cursory glance over the religious landscapes of Asia and the Americas in the wake of European colonial expansion, for example, turns up dozens of examples of religious movements that took their framework from Christianity but filled in all the details with material drawn from native traditions. That's what happens, very often, when people find themselves confronted by a powerful, successful, and appealing foreign culture but still feel a strong attachment to their own cultural heritage: they split the difference and reinvent their own traditions in ways that both pay homage to the foreign culture's ideas and compete with their appeal.

The new version of Judaism that resulted from this process had a rough road ahead of it. The Jews who had not been deported to Babylon rejected the innovations, and the books of Nehemiah and Ezra—the last two historical books of the Old Testament—describe the firm and, at times, violent resistance faced by the returning exiles. Still, due at least in part to the backing of the Persian government, the exiles and their ideas won out. The Temple was rebuilt, the newly codified scriptures became central to Jewish religious life, and Judah settled down to enjoy three centuries of relative tranquility.

How much of Zarathustra's apocalyptic ideology Judaism absorbed from Persian sources at this stage of its history is an open question. The basic elements of the apocalypse meme, though, must have found a home in at least some small corners of Judaism. The evidence for this is simply that when times changed, and the Jews once again found themselves facing national catastrophe, one consequence was the birth of a dramatically new form of apocalyptic narrative that would redefine visions of the future across the Western world for millennia to come.

$$\Omega$$

In 334 BCE, King Alexander of Macedon—a half-barbarian kingdom northwest of Greece, which had conquered Greece itself in the previous generation and now looked east for bigger prey—led his armies across the narrow straits that separated the Greek peninsula from what is now Turkey, and marched straight toward the heart of the Persian Empire. Alexander and his men had scores to settle; Persia had made repeated attempts to conquer Greece in the century or so before his time; the charismatic young monarch, who also happened to be one of the greatest military geniuses in human history, was more or less planning to serve the Persians a good strong dose of their own medicine.

He did much more than that. By the time Alexander drank himself to death in 323 BCE, he was the undisputed ruler of an empire that stretched from the banks of the Nile to the valley of the Indus, and included every scrap of territory once ruled by Persia. He left no heirs, and so the generals of his army did the logical thing and carved up his empire among them. One of them, Seleucus, ended up with the chunk that contained Judah, and his heirs—the Seleucids—solidified their holdings into one of the major power blocs of their time. The Jews thus found themselves abruptly transferred from the domain of a relatively friendly imperial overlord to a new regime that would inaugurate one of the Western world's least pleasant habits.

The heirs of Alexander, in fact, were the people who pioneered cultural chauvinism in the Western tradition. Macedon had adopted Greek culture not that long before Alexander's time, and the Macedonians still had the fervor of the freshly converted; as far as they were concerned, Greek culture was the only culture worth having, and Alexander and most of his generals saw their conquest of the Persian Empire at least partly as an opportunity to spread the blessings of Greek culture to the rest of the world. When anybody showed a lack of enthusiasm for those blessings, the Macedonian response—like those of countless cultural zealots since their time—was to reach for a sword.

This is basically what happened to the Jews. In the province of Judea, as it came to be known, the upper classes quickly found that a working knowledge of Greek language and culture was just as important to getting ahead as the equivalent knowledge of Persian had been before Alexander's conquests, but with the added pressure of a Greek-speaking ruling class that considered all non-Greek culture to be barbarian nonsense. Over the course of the third century BCE, in response to the allurements and pressures of Macedonian rule, a large faction of Jews adopted much of Greek culture, and Greek theaters, gymnasia, and athletic competitions appeared in Jerusalem. Meanwhile, a larger faction of traditionalists rejected all these things, and demanded the abolition of Greek culture and a return to Jewish tradition.

All this came to a head in the early second century BCE. By the time Antiochus IV ascended the throne of the Seleucids in 175 BCE, the cultural struggle in Judea had nearly reached the point of civil war, and the traditionalists—ironically enough, given what happened the last time this had been tried—were busily trying to set up an alliance with Egypt to restore Judea's independence. The threat of an Egyptian invasion supported by a domestic fifth column was not one Antiochus was willing to take lightly. In 168 BCE, he brought an army into Judea and set out to settle the issue once and for all by exterminating Jewish culture, and any Jews who happened to cling to it too tightly, in favor of the heritage of Greece.

A more balanced policy might have enabled Antiochus to broker a peace between the factions and keep Judea in his kingdom. Antiochus was not a balanced man, though, and the atrocities his soldiers inflicted on traditionalist Jews sparked an explosion. A guerrilla army under the command of Judah Maccabee—"Judah the Hammer"—took on the Seleucid forces and, after a brutal four-year war, succeeded in driving them out of Judea and restoring Judea's independence. The Jewish rebels had plenty of ordinary weapons of war, but they also had a secret weapon, one that may well have played a crucial role in winning the struggle for popular support that's crucial for the survival of any guerrilla campaign. That weapon comes down to us in the Bible as the Book of Daniel.

Nobody knows who wrote the stories and prophecies that were later collected to form the Book of Daniel. They take place in Babylon during the period when the Jewish exiles were interned there, but linguistic and historical evidence shows that they were actually written just before or during the Maccabean revolt. It's been argued plausibly that the Babylonian setting was a form of protective camouflage; at a time when open criticism of the Seleucid government and predictions of its fall would have counted as high treason, what better way to conceal them than to pretend to be talking about another oppressor of the Jewish people who had the advantage of being four hundred years dead?

The backdating of the texts was only one level of camouflage, however. The material that went into the Book of Daniel is of two very different types. The first is a series of stories in which Daniel, with the help of the God of his people and his own quick wits, outsmarts a series of gentile kings and defends the Jews. The second and far more explosive type of material is a series of visions sent by God to reveal the future to Daniel. The core theme of the visions is that there will be four great and terrible kingdoms; the last of them will be destroyed by divine intervention, and after that a Jewish monarch will become lord of the world, the dead will come back to life, and an age without suffering will begin and last forever.

This is simply the Zoroastrian prophecy of the Saoshyant transposed into a Jewish key, of course, and the identification is clinched by the fact that just as the Saoshyant was supposed to be descended from the seed of Zarathustra, the Messiah—literally, "anointed one"—who filled the same role in Jewish apocalyptic was supposed to be descended from the seed of David. Still, an important factor entered into the apocalypse meme with the Book of Daniel, and it came from the need for camouflage. The stories of the Saoshyant are written in straightforward terms as simple predictions, but the prophecies in the Book of Daniel are veiled in symbolic imagery of hallucinatory intensity, a nightmare panoply of strange beasts, towering statues, gods on thrones, and angels packing weaponry. Most of the visions are at least partly explained by helpful angels, but there is more than enough ambiguity to keep Macedonian eyes from guessing that what the visions predict is the defeat of Antiochus IV and the restoration of Jewish independence.

That ambiguity carried a heavy burden of consequences for the future. Long after Judah Maccabee became the first king of Judea since Zedekiah's time, the prophecies of Daniel stayed in circulation. Readers found ways to apply the bizarre imagery of Daniel's visions to events the authors of the Daniel texts never anticipated, and new texts found their way into circulation, filling the minds of their readers with even more gaudy predictions of the end of history and the coming of a perfect world. It's among the bitter jests of history that the resulting torrent of apocalyptic literature, originally set in motion by an attempt to save the kingdom of Judea from a foreign oppressor, played a key role in setting the stage for the series of disasters that destroyed Judea utterly and scattered the Jewish people across three continents.

Ω

In 1946, a small group of Bedouin tribesmen happened on a cave in the Wadi Qumran, a dry streambed in the deserts of Jordan not far from the Dead Sea, and noticed seven tattered scrolls lying half buried in the sand and rubble of the cave floor. Knowing that such things were worth money, they took the scrolls and sold them to an antiquities dealer, who realized they were important and brought in the press. Scholars who examined the scrolls quickly determined that they were among the very oldest manuscripts in Hebrew to have survived. Archeologists immediately went to work looking for more scrolls in the same area, and found an abundance of them, and the "Dead Sea Scrolls" began their career as the storm center of a hurricane of academic controversy and scandal.

The first generation or so of scholarship on the Scrolls identified them as writings of the Essenes, a poorly documented sectarian group active in Judea around the time of Christ. That identification came to be widely accepted, in part because most of the Scrolls remained unpublished and untranslated, in the hands of a small group of scholars whose professional status gained immensely from their exclusive access to the texts. Not until 1991 was the logjam finally cleared away, and when this happened it soon became clear that what had surfaced was something far more interesting than the library of a single sect.

The Qumran scrolls, it turned out, represented a broad selection of Jewish religious literature from the first century CE. Roughly a quarter of the total collection consists of copies of books from the Jewish scriptures as they exist today; there are also copies of previously known apocrypha—that is, books that didn't make it into the official collection, but have much in common with the books that did. There are books on astrology and magic, lengthy commentaries on Biblical texts from a variety of viewpoints, several detailed books on a calendar that differs sharply from the one standard in Judaism then and now, and a collection of texts written from the viewpoint of a very distinctive, sectarian Judaism that may well have been that of the ancient Essenes. All in all, the Dead Sea Scrolls provide a fascinating glimpse into the intellectual life of Judea in the century or so that included the lifetime of Christ.

Among the things hardest to miss from that glimpse is the way that the apocalypse meme pervaded Jewish culture at the time. The Book of Daniel is among the Biblical books found among the Scrolls; the apocrypha in the collection include such famous works of Jewish apocalyptic literature as the First Book of Enoch and the Book of Jubilees; and the previously unknown texts include dozens of apocalyptic books. The aptly named War Scroll describes the approaching struggle between good and evil in bloodthirsty terms: "On the day when the Kittim [Romans] fall there shall be a battle and horrible carnage before the God of Israel, for it is a day appointed by him from ancient times as a battle of annihilation for the sons of darkness…The sons of light and the forces of darkness shall fight together to show the strength of God with the roar of a great multitude and the shout of gods and men: a day of disaster."

Evidence from beyond the Qumran caves supports this picture of a Jewish world awash in apocalyptic frenzy. Flavius Josephus, who commanded Jewish armies in the revolt against Rome that began in 66 CE, was captured by the Romans, and switched sides when it became clear who was going to win, described Judea on the brink of the revolt in exactly these terms. His book *On the Jewish War* paints a portrait of a bitterly divided society, split among Pharisees who embraced most of Zarathustra's ideas, Sadducee traditionalists who rejected them, Essenes who withdrew from society to pursue their own salvation, and Zealots who interpreted the apocalypse meme in purely political terms and hoped to launch a second Maccabean revolt against the power of Rome. The country seethed with prophets and rabble-rousers proclaiming the imminent arrival of the End Times.

Eventually, with the help of decades of mismanagement at the hands of a series of corrupt Roman colonial officials, the Zealots got their wish. A minor quarrel in 66 CE between Greeks and Jews in the coastal city of Caesarea provided the spark for rebellion, but it could have been almost anything. By then a great many, perhaps a majority, of the Jewish people in Judea and elsewhere expected the arrival of the promised Messiah and the overthrow of Rome, and the voices of those who tried to address the crisis in reasonable terms were drowned out by the shouts of those whose minds were so full of the apocalypse meme that there was no room for anything else.

The Roman response was quick and devastating. In 66, a first attempt by local Roman officials to quell the rebellion with troops on hand fizzled, but the next year the experienced Roman general Vespasian arrived on the scene with four veteran legions. By the start of 68, after heavy fighting, the northern half of Judea was back in Roman hands, and the legions began to move south. A sudden political crisis in Rome—the overthrow and suicide of the emperor Nero, and the quick rise and fall of three successors—took up most of Vespasian's attention for the following year, but the crisis ended unexpectedly in 69 with Vespasian himself mounting the imperial throne. His son Titus took command of the Roman forces in Judea, marched on Jerusalem, and took it in 70 after a bitter siege. Josephus later estimated that 1,100,000 people died during the siege, most of them from hunger, disease, and the brutal political infighting among the leaders of the Jewish rebellion, while another 97,000 were captured and sold as slaves by the victorious Romans. Mopping-up operations kept the Roman army busy for two more years, but the fall of Masada, the last Jewish stronghold, in 72 ended the revolt.

The same political passions and apocalyptic dreams that sparked the rising of 66 CE, though, remained at white heat in the Jewish community. In 115, as the emperor Trajan marched east to battle the Parthian Empire—the successors of the old Persians—Jewish communities in North Africa rose in rebellion and slaughtered their gentile neighbors. The fighting spread to Judea before Trajan returned and the revolt was crushed by his legions.

Finally, in 132, a third major rising headed by Simon Bar Kokhba flared across Judea. This time the Romans pretty clearly decided to settle the matter once and for all. Fifteen legions converged on the rebel province from as far away as the Danube River. After three years of carnage, the revolt was flattened, along with most of Judea, and all but a tiny remnant of the Jewish population was killed, sold into slavery, or driven into exile. A new city, Aelia Capitolina, was built atop the ruins of Jerusalem, and Jews were forbidden to enter it on pain of death.

This was presumably not the future imagined by the apocalyptic dreamers whose words played so large a role in sparking the violence. The War Scroll, as it turned out, was quite correct to call the struggle between the Jews and the Romans "a day of disaster," but it failed to predict one crucial detail: the disaster landed almost entirely on the heads of the Jewish people.

Ω

The survivors of the three great rebellions ended up scattered across most of the known world. Over the next few centuries, they reworked their religious traditions, drawing mostly on the teachings of the Pharisees to create the Judaism that exists today. The experiences of their ancestors in Babylon provided them with a template for the demands of survival in exile, and it served the Jewish people well; the work of the generations of rabbis who created the Talmud, the great collection of Jewish religious law and custom, created a faith and a community structure capable of surviving almost anything the rest of the world could throw at it.

The rest of the world, unfortunately, was more than happy to oblige. In those parts of the Roman and Parthian

Empires that fell under Muslim control at the time of the great Arab conquests of the seventh and eighth centuries CE, Jewish communities did relatively well. Muslim law and custom gave Jews the right to continue to practice their religion, though it also authorized the Muslim authorities to place heavy taxes on them. In what had been the European provinces of the Roman Empire, where the Christian religion came to dominate society, however, the position of the Jews was a good deal more precarious. Until around the year 1000, the newborn nations of Europe had to struggle for survival against invaders from three directions—Muslim armies probing up from the south, Viking raiders sailing down from the north, and nomadic tribes migrating out of central Asia to the east. The scattered Jewish population of Europe suffered from the impact of these invasions along with their Christian neighbors.

By the turn of the millennium, these pressures had transformed European Christianity into a warrior faith and driven the emergence of a feudal military tradition more than capable of holding its own in a violent world. As it rounded on its former invaders, the new European order turned with equal ferocity against Europe's own dissident populations, and Jews were high on that list. In 1096, as armies assembled across Europe to turn the tables on the Muslim world in the First Crusade, peasant soldiers in the Rhine valley began to massacre the Jewish population in every town they passed. Between four and eight thousand Jews were slaughtered by the time the Crusaders finally went on toward the Holy Land.

The same thing happened in 1146, when the Second Crusade was being organized, and it happened during the buildup to every subsequent Crusade as well. The link between the Crusader ideal and mob violence against Jews became so deeply rooted in European culture that most of a millennium later, in the nineteenth century, pogroms against Jews in eastern Europe were still being carried out by mobs chanting the word "Hep"—short for *Hierosolyma est perdita*, "Jerusalem is lost" in Latin.

These horrific events breathed new life into the apocalyptic side of the Jewish tradition. The dream of a glorious future in which the Messiah would finally appear and lead the Jewish people back to their Middle Eastern homeland became one of the few consolations left to European Jews at a time when they risked being beaten or butchered by Christian mobs at any moment. In the wake of the worst outbreaks, too, bands of Jewish survivors left their devastated homes and began the long journey toward Jerusalem convinced that the Messiah would be waiting for them when they arrived. A few completed the journey, and became part of the Jewish population of Palestine; most died on the way.

Every so often, in turn, someone in the Jewish community would declare himself the Messiah or a prophet announcing the Messiah's arrival, and gather a following among desperate Jews. According to the medieval Jewish author Moses Maimonides, a French Jew did this the year after the massacres of 1086, and was put to death by the French; Maimonides does not mention the would-be Messiah's name, and no other record survives of his activities. Around 1280, the mystic Abraham Abulafia proclaimed himself the Messiah and announced 1290 as the date his reign would begin; in 1295, in the town of Avila in Spain, Nissim ben Abraham proclaimed the imminent arrival of the Messianic kingdom; around the beginning of the fifteenth century, in the Spanish town of Cisneros, Moses Botarel revealed himself as the Messiah; in 1502, near Venice, it was the turn of Asher Lämmlein, who attracted a great following with his proclamation that the Messiah would arrive within six months if the Jewish community repented of its sins and practiced charity and asceticism.

The most spectacular of the false Messiahs of medieval Judaism, though, was Sabbatai Zevi. Born to a prosperous Jewish family in the town of Smyrna in Turkey in 1626, Zevi became a student of the Kabbalah, the mystical tradition of Judaism, and encountered a prophecy—extracted from the Zohar, the most important Kabbalistic text—that claimed that the Messiah would reveal himself in 1648. Not long after his twentieth birthday, Zevi became convinced that he was the Messiah, and began to proclaim his mission to his fellow Jews. Expelled from the Jewish community of Smyrna for these claims, he moved from town to town, gradually attracting a following and a reputation as a miracle worker and holy ascetic.

Within a decade or so, Zevi had become a seventeenth-century superstar with followers on three continents and a capable public relations manager, the Kabbalist rabbi Nathan of Gaza, who kept the newfangled printing presses of the Jewish community busy turning out broadsheets and pamphlets backing Zevi's Messianic claims. Zevi's wife Sarah was a star in her own right—orphaned in childhood by a Christian mob, forcibly baptized, and put into a convent, she escaped the nuns in her teen years, fled to the Jewish community in Amsterdam, and supported herself by prostitution for a time before becoming convinced that she was destined to marry the Messiah. Zevi announced that just as the prophet Hosea had married a "woman of whoredom," he himself was destined to marry an unchaste woman; the fact that by all accounts Sarah was a beautiful and charming young woman may not have been unrelated to his decision.

In 1665, Zevi had his Messiahship formally announced in the synagogue in Smyrna, and the news spread like wildfire across Europe, western Asia, and North Africa. The entire Jewish population of the town of Avignon in France made arrangements to move en masse to Palestine to take part in the messianic kingdom, while tens of thousands of individual Jews made the same decision and headed toward Jerusalem. As word spread that Zevi had instructed his followers to give up many traditional Jewish customs and to celebrate on days that had been formerly set aside for mourning—all things that, according to some accounts, the Messiah was expected to do—Jewish communities over much of the world polarized into pro- and anti-Zevi parties, and even Christians and Muslims began to listen to the debates with some interest.

The Turkish government was also interested in Zevi,

though their motivations were far more pragmatic. Concerned that the movement that was springing up around Zevi might all too easily turn political, or even revolutionary, the Turks had Zevi arrested and imprisoned at Abydos, far from his followers. This had no effect on the movement; many of Zevi's adherents went at once to Abydos and treated the prison as though it was Zevi's royal court. At length the Turks had had enough; Zevi was taken in chains to Istanbul and offered the straightforward choice between converting to Islam and having his head cut off. After considering the matter, Zevi decided to abandon his religion to save his life.

The news of his conversion was splashed across the mass media of the time and left the hopes of his followers devastated. A minority of them managed to convince themselves that Zevi was still the Messiah, and meant to communicate some profound and mystical teaching by his act; many of these ended up converting to Islam themselves, forming a sect called the Donmeh which still exists in Turkey. Most of his followers crept back to their homes and endured the mockery and condemnation of their neighbors.

There were other would-be Messiahs after Sabbatai Zevi, though none who managed so spectacular a rise and so sorry a fall. The most recent candidate, at least in the eyes of many of his followers, was Rabbi Menachem Schneerson, who headed the orthodox Chabad Lubavitch movement from 1951 until his death in 1994. The "Lubavitcher Rebbe," as he was generally known, made no public claim to Messiahship, and whether he circulated such claims in private is a matter of heated controversy in some circles. Nonetheless, a significant number of his followers convinced themselves that the Rebbe was destined to fulfill the old messianic dream, and in the years since his death a faction continues to insist that he will rise from the dead someday soon and proclaim himself as the Messiah.

Still, long before these medieval and modern would-be Messiahs, the apocalypse meme had found an even more effective carrier, one that would spread it around the world. It's all the more intriguing that this carrier was founded by a figure that most Jews, from his time to ours, consider to be yet another false Messiah—the dissident Galilean rabbi from Nazareth that later generations of his followers came to call Jesus Christ.

CHAPTER THREE:

WAITING FOR THE ANTICHRIST

On a spring day not quite two thousand years ago, a Jewish religious teacher and a handful of his followers climbed up onto the Mount of Olives, just outside of Jerusalem. Earlier that day, they had been to the Temple of Jerusalem, and the teacher had told his startled listeners that soon not one stone of all the temple buildings would be left standing. Now, as they sat on the weathered limestone of the Mount, with its splendid view of the Jordan valley, his inner circle of students asked their teacher about the catastrophe he had predicted.

It would come soon, the teacher told them. There would be wars and rumors of wars, famines and plagues and earthquakes in various corners of the world, but his students were not to be frightened. There would be plenty of people claiming to be the promised Messiah, but his followers were not to believe any of them. The sign they were to watch for was the setting up of the statue of a pagan god—"the abomination of desolation," in Daniel's phrase—in the Temple, as in the time of the Maccabees. When that happened, it would be time to flee into the hills at once, not even delaying long enough to gather up their possessions. The destruction would be total, the death toll horrific, but it would be over in a short time, and after that, the Son of Man would come into his kingdom. All of this would happen very soon, he stressed—soon enough that some of the people who were alive at that moment would see it happen.

He was, as it turns out, absolutely right. As described in Chapter Two, the years leading up to the Jewish rebellion against Rome in 66 AD were troubled times, full of "wars and rumors of wars," as well as apocalyptic claims and would-be Messiahs seeking the redemption of Israel by peaceful or violent means. When the rebellion finally broke out, the Roman Empire responded with overwhelming force, and murderous struggles among the Jewish defenders added to the carnage. By the time the fighting was over, Judea had been ravaged from one end to the other, Jerusalem and its Temple were smoking ruins, and most of the former Jewish population of Judea had become casualties, slaves, or refugees. In the wake of the cataclysm, finally, the newly founded faith of Christianity began to find converts across the Roman world: the Son of Man had indeed come into his kingdom. As prophecies go, this one was a solid hit.

Ω

Around the time that the rubble of Jerusalem finally stopped smoldering, a follower of this same Jewish teacher, while staying on the island of Patmos in the eastern Mediterranean, had an even more spectacular head-on collision with the future. His name was Yochanan, a Hebrew name that has passed through several other languages to become the English name "John." Very little more is known about him, though rumors from a long ways back insist he was the same person who wrote the Gospel of John. One Sunday—he mentions this detail—a wave of terrifying visionary imagery broke over his head, and he transcribed it all in what is now the last and weirdest book of the Bible, the Book of Revelation.

John's vision is so packed with action and strangeness that it's almost impossible to summarize in any meaningful way, but the attempt has to be made. The book starts off with a vision of Jesus with white hair, seven stars in his hand, and a double-edged sword sticking out of his mouth, standing in the middle of seven candlesticks and passing on messages to the seven Christian churches in Asia Minor. Then a door opens in heaven and John plunges into the heart of his vision. There are luminous figures and books sealed with seven seals, monstrous beasts rising out of the ocean, a woman clothed in the sun and a lamb with seven horns and seven eyes, a scarlet-clad whore riding on the back of a monster, stars falling into the sea, trumpets sounding, and a body count extreme even by the standards of a Hollywood global-catastrophe thriller.

Still, there is a central thread to all this baroque imagery. The forces of evil in the world emanate from a city on seven hills, the political and economic center of the world, ruled by a monarch who demands that all people worship him as a god. To this city and its empire, John predicts, a string of unparalleled disasters are coming. There will be earthquakes and epidemics, wars and invasions, and the followers of Christ will be persecuted savagely. Horsemen in iron breastplates, compared by John to locusts and scorpions, will sweep across the landscape bringing death and terror. In a series of cataclysmic battles, the forces of Babylon will be routed and the kingdom of Christ established on its ruins. For a thousand years—the Millennium—that kingdom will endure, and then the powers of evil will be released again for a time; the four quarters of the world will go to war against one another, the mysterious kingdom of Gog in the far north will rally to the side of Satan and be defeated along with the Prince of Darkness, and then a new heaven and a new earth will appear and a luminous city of jewels hover in the sky.

Translate it out of the language of Jewish apocalyptic symbolism and John's message is clear. He calls the city on seven hills Babylon, but it's instantly recognizable as Rome—among other details, the actual city of Babylon isn't built on seven hills, while Rome famously is. The emperors of Rome did indeed require citizens of the empire to worship them as gods, and persecuted Christians for refusing to do so. The same language of imagery the author of the Book of Daniel used to predict the end of the Seleucid Greek rule over Judea, in other words, was adapted by John to predict the decline and fall of the Roman Empire.

The astonishing detail is that he was right. The Roman Empire was, in fact, ravaged by epidemics and earthquakes in the three centuries between John's vision and the fall of Rome. The terrifying horsemen showed up on schedule—historians call them the Huns—and so did the battles, as the Roman Empire was wracked by barbarian invasions and civil war. For a thousand years after the Christianization of the Roman Empire, Christianity was the unchallenged faith of the Western world. Thereafter the devil, in the form of classical Greek and Roman culture, did indeed get let out of prison; we call that period the Renaissance. The last phases of John's vision are harder to fit with what happened after the Renaissance, granted, but even a very good prophet has his off days.

Even with that last caveat, John's vision counts as one of the most spectacularly successful prophecies on record. At a time when nobody in his right mind imagined the fall of Rome's mighty empire and the rise to power of the despised and marginal sect of Christianity, he predicted both, along with a flurry of other details that make sense in the context of the centuries that followed his time. Thus it's all the more telling that only a small minority of Christians have ever accepted what has been called the preterist interpretation of the prophecies of Jesus and John—that is, the recognition that they have already come true. The majority have rejected this in order to turn both prophecies into raw material for the apocalypse meme.

Ω

One of the most lively debates in contemporary Christian historical studies has focused on whether Jesus of Nazareth himself was a believer in that meme. Since Albert Schweitzer's *The Quest of the Historical Jesus* launched historical questions about the origins of Christianity out of the academy a hundred years ago and gave them a place in popular culture, a majority of scholars have argued that the account given in the Gospels is roughly correct, and Jesus spent much of his public career preaching that the end of the world was about to happen. Still, the minority that has argued for the opposite view has had powerful ammunition on its side.

One forceful case against an apocalyptically minded Jesus was made by Stevan L. Davies in a 1983 study of the Gospel of Thomas, one of the so-called "Gnostic gospels" found in the Egyptian desert at Nag Hammadi in 1945. While most scholarship on the Gospel of Thomas argued that it was a late Gnostic forgery, Davies presented strong evidence that it was instead a very early source—at least as early as "Q," the laboriously reconstructed common source used by Mark and Luke as raw material for their gospels—and that standard "form criticism" methods show that the versions of many of Jesus's sayings in the Gospel of Thomas are probably closer to the original than those of the official gospels.

What makes this evidence challenging is that the Jesus portrayed in the Gospel of Thomas says nothing about the end of the world. He speaks of the Kingdom of Heaven, but that kingdom is not something that can be expected to show up with an apocalyptic bang. It comes into being within the soul of the individual who is awakened by Jesus's words: "The kingdom of Heaven is within you." The drumbeat of apocalyptic predictions that fills so much space in the official gospels is nowhere in Thomas. Davies argued, partly on this basis, that Thomas was compiled before the cataclysm of 70 CE, and that the apocalyptic elements in Christianity were inserted into the faith by the generation of Christian believers living immediately afterward. Unpopular when Davies wrote, this view has become more widely accepted since then, winning support from such major Biblical scholars as Marvin Meyer.

Whether or not apocalyptic ideas played any role in Jesus's own teachings, though, they very quickly became central to the new Christian religion as it separated itself from Judaism and found its own niche in the bustling religious marketplace of the classical Mediterranean world. The persecutions that Roman authority inflicted on Christians, and Christians not long thereafter inflicted on one another, did as much to assure the place of apocalyptic in Christian thought as other persecutions had done to fuse it into the foundations of Judaism. Unlike its parent faith, however, Christianity was an aggressively missionary religion, and, as it chased converts across the length and breadth of the Old World, it spread the apocalypse meme with it. As the

Christian faith rose to power in the wake of Rome's decline and fall, in turn, the meme rose with it.

Ω

Not too many years ago, popular histories of the Middle Ages used to insist that the greatest of all mass panics swept through Europe just before the year 1000, as people across medieval Europe convinced themselves that the world was about to end. Fields went untended, craftsmen walked away from their jobs, and life ground to a halt, so the story went, as belief in the imminent Second Coming of Christ made all worldly activities seem like a waste of time.

The historians who were responsible for creating this legend, it turns out, hadn't done their homework. It was quite true that a great many people in the late 990s expected the turn of the millennium to bring about the end of the world, but it was just as true that every other decade between the fall of Rome and the Industrial Revolution was awash with its own apocalyptic speculations and had its own preferred dates for the end. Nor was Christianity unique in fostering a bumper crop of apocalyptic beliefs during these years; while Christians waited for the Second Coming, their Jewish neighbors built a rich structure of folk beliefs around what would happen when the Messiah finally arrived, while the Muslims with whom Christian Europeans traded, fought, and studied developed their own elaborate speculations about the End of Days.

For most of those centuries, the Christian versions of the

apocalypse meme shared a common sense of time based on a particular interpretation of the Bible. Well before the fall of Rome, in fact, Christians had come up with what for centuries thereafter was the standard chronology for the end of the world. The key to their analysis was 2 Peter 3:8—"But, beloved, be not ignorant of this one thing, that one day is with the Lord as a thousand years, and a thousand years as one day." This equation was then applied to the Book of Genesis, and convinced most medieval Christians that the seven days of Creation were seven thousand years, of which the last was the millennium mentioned in the Book of Revelation. Everyone assumed that their own time was somewhere toward the end of the sixth millennium; all a would-be prophet had to do was figure out just where, and timing the events of Revelation was a cinch.

Of course figuring out exactly where the current year falls in that scenario proved to be the difficulty, but the failure of each calculation simply inspired other prophets to try again. In the earliest years of the Church, when the Second Coming was expected on a daily basis, the birth of Jesus was fixed somewhere right up against the end of the sixth millennium. Later on, when a couple of centuries had passed since the Crucifixion, students of scripture struggled to come up with reasons to place Jesus's birth in the middle of the sixth millennium, so that the Second Coming could occur sometime very soon.

Hilarian, a bishop in North Africa, settled on this date in 397 in his book *The Progress of Time*, and announced that the final battle between Christ and the Antichrist was exactly

101 years away. Not all of Hilarian's contemporaries were willing to wait that long. Sulpicius Severus, the close friend and biographer of St. Martin of Tours, writing around the same year that Hilarian's prophecy saw the light of day, mentioned that the saint had told him seven years previously that the Antichrist had already been born and was a child, and would seize world power as soon as he reached adulthood. "Ponder," he wrote, "how close these coming fearful events are!"

By the time it was clear the fearful events weren't going to happen on St. Martin's schedule, new calculations were forthcoming. One example was the work of Beatus of Liébana, a Spanish monk who lived in the eighth century, and who set out to calculate the year the sixth millennium would end by adding up all the dates in the Bible. He reckoned the period from the creation of Adam to the birth of Christ as 5,227 years, and since he was writing in 786 CE, it was easy to demonstrate that the sixth millennium would end and the Antichrist appear in the year 800, a mere fourteen years away.

The flurry of apocalyptic claims that focused on the year 1000 therefore appeared against a background of many other prophecies of imminent doom, and when the predictions centered on 1000 failed in their turn, plenty of new predictions were forthcoming. The great struggle between the Papacy and the Holy Roman Empire that convulsed medieval Europe in the eleventh and twelfth centuries accordingly spawned plenty of claims that either the Pope or the Emperor was the Antichrist. When those struggles resumed in the early thirteenth century with the canny and colorful Emperor Frederick II as the imperial protagonist, these same speculations came surging back, louder than before.

As that latter quarrel proceeded, the Pope and his partisans unleashed broadside after broadside claiming that the Bible's description of the Antichrist fit Frederick to a hair. Frederick's publicists—yes, medieval Holy Roman Emperors had their own public relations people—responded with equally convincing arguments that the Antichrist predicted in the Bible was obviously the description of a Pope. While Frederick died unexpectedly in 1250, disappointing true believers on both sides of the controversy, the arguments that his publicists invented went on to have a remarkable career of their own. They were wielded repeatedly as a weapon against Rome before, during, and after the Reformation, and still appear routinely in the more anti-Catholic end of Protestant apocalyptic literature.

Ω

People in the time of Frederick II knew exactly what to expect from a potential Antichrist, too. A series of increasingly detailed biographies-in-advance of the great villain of the Book of Revelation appeared in the early Middle Ages, filling out the vague outline provided by the Bible with a wealth of colorful anecdotes. Adso of Melk, whose life of the Antichrist was the most popular of these and became the model for nearly all later writings on the subject, earned his role as the Beast's premier biographer by drawing inspiration from the life stories of saints, or hagiographies, that formed a major publishing phenomenon in his time.

Hagiographies were not biographies in the modern sense of the word. They focused on describing the kind of life a saint was supposed to live, rather than worrying overmuch about the facts. Adso realized that the same logic could be applied just as well to the career of the ultimate anti-saint. The result, the *Letter on the Antichrist*, was published in 950 and dedicated to Queen Gerberga, the wife of King Louis IV of France. By the standards of the time, which admittedly was an age in which most people couldn't read and every copy of a book had to be written out by hand, it became a bestseller and retained that status for many centuries.

According to Adso, the Antichrist would be a Jew, belonging to the tribe of Dan. He would be conceived in the usual way, rather than by some diabolical equivalent of the Virgin Birth, but his mother would be the wickedest woman in all of history; she would be possessed by Satan himself before, during, and after the Antichrist's conception. The child thus conceived, Adso went on, would grow up proud, rich, and famous, and would become a teacher, instructing people to practice vices instead of virtues and to worship demons instead of God.

The Antichrist would begin his career with bribery and corruption, spreading his vast wealth as gifts to seduce people into his service. To convert those who were not susceptible to bribes, he would perform miracles with Satan's help, while those who resisted both these lures, as his power increased, would be tortured and killed. Finally, as the Antichrist's rule over the world became total, every faithful Christian who could be tracked down by the agents of the Antichrist would be forced to choose between renouncing God and being put to some horrible death.

For three and a half years, then, the Antichrist would reign unchallenged, but his final defeat would be sudden and merciless. According to the learned, said Adso, the Antichrist would be seated on his throne in his pavilion on the Mount of Olives in Jerusalem, when all of a sudden Christ would return and "slay him with the breath of His mouth." There was apparently some disagreement in Adso's sources whether Christ would do this directly, or whether the Archangel Michael would serve as point man for the divine hit squad. One way or another, though, the Antichrist would be annihilated; there would then be a forty-day interval for those Christians who had been led astray by the Antichrist to repent and do penance, and then the Last Judgment would happen and time would end once and for all.

Much of the material Adso and the other medieval biographers of the Antichrist used to fill out the story of their not-yet-born subject was simply made up out of whole cloth, but not all. Adso in particular was a capable scholar by the standards of his time, and ransacked the Bible and the handful of scriptural commentaries that could be gotten in France in the Dark Ages for details he could weave into his narrative. Still, there was another important source, which has been finessed by most scholarship on the subject.

At the heart of Christianity is the belief that Jesus of

Nazareth had been the expected Jewish Messiah. The Jews disagreed, of course, and their beliefs about the Messiah that they expected had very little in common with Christian ideas on the same subject. From a medieval Christian perspective, it was a simple and logical step to claim that the Jews were waiting, not for the Messiah, but for his opposite, and Jewish traditions about the Messiah thus became a covert but central source for Christian ideas about the Antichrist. A good deal of the long and sordid history of Christian anti-Semitism has at least some of its roots in that identification. To medieval Christians, after all, the equation between their Antichrist and the Messiah expected by the Jews meant that the Jews in their midst were not merely practicing a different religion but waiting around for the chance to serve the powers of ultimate evil.

Adso's work thus cast a long shadow. It was enormously influential, then and later, and you can still find plenty of accounts of the Antichrist's expected career that take most of their details from *Letter on the Antichrist*, usually without knowing it. Two other figures popular in medieval versions of the End Times, though, have vanished from recent narratives. One of them was already much discussed in Adso's own time, and found his way into *Letter on the Antichrist*: the Last Emperor.

The dream of a heroic Roman emperor who would reestablish the peace and prosperity of the fallen empire went back a very long way. Prophetic writings dating from long before Adso's time wove that dream together with the Book of Revelation to predict a final Emperor who would vanquish the Muslims, restore the Holy Land to Christian control, and bring peace to the world for a fleeting interval before the advent of the Antichrist. Most of these earlier writings assumed that the Last Emperor would be the ruler of the Byzantine Empire, that fragment of the old Roman state that survived straight through the Middle Ages in what is now Greece and Turkey. Adso displayed his penchant for originality here, though, by redefining the Last Emperor as a French king, one of the heirs of Charlemagne.

Adso didn't manage to find a place for the second medieval End Times figure, for this latter wasn't invented until many years after his time. During the thirteenth century, many of the hopes that once clustered around the Last Emperor found a new focus in the Angelic Pope, who was supposed to appear in time to lead the church through a final reform just before the end of the world. This new figure came with an edge, however, for he was more or less defined as everything that the popes of the Middle Ages claimed to be and weren't. The Angelic Pope, many writers of the time insisted, would be a saintly man who would restore the church to a condition of moral virtue and holy poverty. This rhetoric took shape in response to the overt corruption of the medieval Church, but it also drew on the work of one of the most innovative minds of the age, a man whose writing would shape apocalyptic beliefs in profound ways long after the Middle Ages were over.

Ω

Joachim of Fiore was born in the Italian province of Calabria around 1135. He had a minor career in the Sicilian civil service, and then underwent a religious conversion and became a Benedictine monk in 1171. In 1184, while traveling to Rome on monastery business, he stopped at the monastery of Casamari, just south of Rome; while he was staying there he had a series of visions that showed him the secret meaning of the Book of Revelation and catapulted him into a new life as an internationally famous prophet. He kept on writing and preaching about the future to a Europewide audience until his death in 1202.

It's difficult to summarize Joachim's visions in any useful way, and even harder to do so with the theory of history that came out of them, both because of the extreme complexity of Joachim's visions and because his thought was shaped by medieval ideas radically different from the ways of thinking most modern people use to interpret the world. Still, the basic concept of Joachim's theory was that the Trinity—the threefold Christian godhead of Father, Son, and Holy Spirit—provided the framework upon which everything in creation took shape, including the whole course of the world's history.

Thus, according to Joachim, there had been an Age of the Father, or Age of Law, running from the creation of the world to the birth of Jesus and corresponding to the Old Testament. There was an Age of the Son, the Age of Grace, running from the birth of Jesus to the downfall of the

Antichrist, which either Joachim or his students—the evidence isn't quite clear one way or the other—predicted would happen right around the year 1260. Finally, there would be an Age of the Holy Spirit, or Age of Liberty, which would begin shortly thereafter and continue until the world actually ended for good sometime in the distant future.

Joachim's theories covered a great deal more than this. He worked out a scheme whereby the Old and New Testament periods were each divided into seven sections that moved in synch with one another, so that the remaining years of the Age of the Son could be predicted in detail on the basis of what had happened in the last century or so of the Age of the Father. When King Richard the Lionheart stopped at Joachim's monastery on his way to the Third Crusade, Joachim accordingly consulted his calculations and informed the king that the Crusade would be a great success and Jerusalem would be liberated from the Saracens. He was quite wrong, and he made a good many other predictions that failed just as completely, but in the usual way these missteps failed to dent his reputation among his contemporaries.

What made Joachim so popular in his time, and so influential for the future, was that his version of the apocalypse meme was essentially optimistic. He made room for the Antichrist and the rest of the hardware of the Book of Revelation, but saw the fireworks of the apocalypse simply as a slightly rough transition between the troubled Age of the Son and a blissful future Age of the Holy Spirit, in which religious and secular institutions would wither away, and the world would become one big monastery where everyone would spend their days in rapt contemplation of God. In theological language made popular in the twentieth century by conservative philosopher Eric Voegelin, Joachim "immanentized the eschaton"—that is, he shifted heaven's bliss out of the otherworldly status that Christian theology had always assigned to it, and revisioned it as a state that could be attained right here on Earth. It was a novel idea in Joachim's time, but would be picked up and used repeatedly over the centuries to come.

Ω

Joachim's immediate impact was on the political and religious quarrels of his own time. The monastic order he founded, the Florensians, went all out to promote his ideas, and the much larger Franciscan order also found plenty to like in Joachim's claim that a new order of "spiritual men" would play a central role in the transition to the Age of the Holy Spirit. Conservative forces in the Catholic Church accordingly found Joachim a convenient target in their struggle against the more liberal Franciscans, and Joachim's teachings on the Trinity were condemned as heretical at the fourth Lateran Council in 1215.

This turned out to be a catastrophic mistake for the conservatives, though its full impact would not be felt for centuries to come. The immediate result was to push the radical wing of the Franciscan order, the Spiritual Franciscans, deeper into opposition to the hierarchy at Rome. The Spirituals were already deeply troubled by the decision made by their order to quietly abandon the tradition of absolute poverty established by their founder, St. Francis of Assisi, and with other moves that brought the Franciscan order more into line with the older monastic bodies whose approach Francis had rejected.

The Church's condemnation of Joachim of Flores added to the pressures that made many Spirituals decide that the Catholic hierarchy was becoming the enemy of their Christian faith. In coming to this belief, they were likely helped by the torrent of anti-Papal propaganda being issued all through the first half of the thirteenth century, as already mentioned, by the supporters of the Emperor Frederick II. Still, an even greater role was played by the harsh response of the Church. Under Pope John XXII, the Spiritual Franciscans were declared heretical, and those who refused to renounce their belief in apostolic poverty were handed over to the Inquisition. This overreaction forced many more moderate Franciscans, and a great many other Catholics as well, to start asking hard questions about the Church—and plenty of these drew on the apocalypse meme and spawned new predictions of imminent doom and deliverance.

In the wake of the persecution of the Spirituals, though, a new theme entered the discussion. Earlier prophets left the task of doing battle with the Antichrist up to God, but at this point there began to be heard calls for mere human beings to do battle with the forces of evil—and not in a metaphorical sense, either. Around 1260, an illiterate Italian prophet named Gerard Segarelli began to preach apostolic poverty and to denounce the Church for its sins, and gathered a large following. In 1300 he was seized by the Inquisition and burned at the stake, but a new leader—Fra Dolcino, the illegitimate son of a priest from Novara—took charge of the group and proclaimed a holy war against the Church. By 1304 the Apostolic Brethren, as they were by this time called, had retreated into the Alps and were carrying on a guerrilla war against the forces of orthodoxy. They were finally defeated in a pitched battle at Monte Rebello in 1307, and Dolcino and many of his followers were tortured to death by the victors, but pockets of Apostolic Brethren held out in isolated Alpine valleys for years thereafter.

Not all apocalyptic movements in medieval Europe were anything like as violent as the Apostolic Brethren. The Brotherhood of the Free Spirit, a movement that attracted enthusiastic followers and violent repression across Europe from the thirteenth century onwards, took the opposite tack; like another counterculture many centuries later, they wanted to make love, not war. Like most medieval heresies, the Free Spirit message was spread by a loose network of wandering prophets, many of them unfrocked priests and monks, but these prophets preached their unique gospel mostly to unmarried women and widows in the wealthy urban classes of medieval society.

That was the key to the movement's success. In medieval Europe, the constant drain of men into the (officially, at least) celibate clergy meant that a very large faction of women remained unmarried, or were married while young to elderly husbands and then faced most of a lifetime of widowhood. Among the nobility and peasantry, the established classes of medieval society, there were socially accepted roles available for unmarried women—for peasants, a wide range of rural trades that were informally reserved for women; for noblewomen, positions as ladies in waiting in the sprawling aristocratic households of the time—but the rising urban professional classes had no such arrangements, and the nunneries could only afford to take a fraction of the resulting surplus. Faced with the prospect of a life of enforced idleness and celibacy, many unmarried women and widows among the urban well-to-do turned either to mystical religion or to illicit love affairs. The advantage of the Free Spirit was that it allowed them to do both at once.

This convenient arrangement was possible because the teachings of the Free Spirit reworked Joachim's vision of an impending Third Age in a distinctly unmonastic way. According to Free Spirit doctrines, in the new age the whole world would return to the condition of Paradise before the fall. Free at last of the burden of original sin, humanity would once again be naked and unashamed, living without labor or sorrow according to a new law, which would be the law of love. Unsurprisingly, that law was interpreted in a robustly physical sense, and easy promiscuity was therefore standard practice among believers in the sect, as was group worship in the nude. The prophets of the Free Spirit also taught that in the Third Age, all property would be shared freely by everyone; in practice, since the prophets were generally poor and their converts were often quite rich, the great majority of the sharing went in one direction.

There was, to be fair, more to the Brotherhood of the Free Spirit than this. Surviving documents of the movement, notably Marguerite de Porete's *Mirror of Simple Souls*, worked out a complex theology on the foundation of the basic Free Spirit ideas, and sketched out a training program for Free Spirit adepts of both sexes in which a period of harsh discipline and deprivation taught the soul to recognize its freedom from material things, after which it could enjoy them freely without guilt. That these ideas were not always simply justifications for the fleshly appeals of the Free Spirit lifestyle is shown by the courage and serenity shown by many Free Spirit adherents when they were condemned to death and burnt at the stake.

Now and then a Free Spirit leader, inevitably male, would publicly proclaim himself the Second Adam and announce the arrival of the Third Age. He and his followers, mostly female, would proceed to act accordingly until the Inquisition caught up with them and burnt them. In between such outbreaks, Free Spirit groups operated underground, meeting secretly in the homes of trusted members and spreading by way of personal contacts. Despite the efforts of the Catholic hierarchy to terminate it with extreme prejudice, the movement had enough appeal to spread over most of Europe and endure for at least five centuries. Its legacy lasted longer still; the belief in an apocalyptic Utopia consisting mostly of sex, nudity, and freedom from having to work for a living became a lasting theme in Western culture, and has cropped up in one form or another in every generation up to the present.

Ω

Until 1415, most apocalyptic movements in European Christianity were as easily contained as the Apostolic Brethren and the Brotherhood of the Free Spirit. In that year, however, the Bohemian priest and teacher Jan Hus was summoned to the Council of Constance on suspicion of heresy. Though he had been promised safe conduct by the Church, he was burned at the stake when he refused to recant his beliefs. This act outraged people throughout what was then the kingdom of Bohemia and is now most of the Czech Republic, and led to even more radical opposition to Rome; when King Wenceslaus IV of Bohemia tried to crack down on the dissenters in 1419, Bohemia exploded into open revolt.

The Hussites, as the rebels came to be called, included a dizzying range of factions from moderates to wild radicals. The radicals—called Taborites for their original meeting place, a mountain they renamed after the Biblical Mount Tabor—borrowed Joachim's prediction of the imminent arrival of the Age of the Holy Spirit, but put militant teeth into the prediction along the lines of Fra Dolcino's Apostolic Brethren. They also had a trump card—a blind general named Jan Žižka, who turned out to be one of the great military geniuses of the age.

Žižka recognized that the Taborite army, which consisted mostly of peasants and was poorly armed by the standards of the time, had to find ways to turn peasant skills to military advantage. His solution was to convert farm wagons into horse-drawn tanks, and use them as fighting vehicles and portable fortifications. Thus equipped, the Taborite forces repeatedly crushed larger enemy armies and raided deep into Germany, forcing a military standoff that won the Bohemian church its independence from Rome. Still, the Taborite millennium failed to arrive, and the Taborites didn't even profit from their victories; they were soundly defeated by conservative forces within Bohemia itself in 1435, and faded from history.

The rhetoric the Taborites borrowed from earlier apocalyptic movements did not fade away so easily, however. In the decades that followed that Taborite defeat, as medieval Christianity moved toward its final crisis, it must often have seemed as though every faction in the turbulent religious politics of the time saw the Antichrist in the faces of its opponents, and insisted on portraying itself as the innocent and persecuted children of God, no matter how poorly its behavior fit that role. Violent attacks on the Catholic hierarchy spawned equally violent reprisals, and when Martin Luther finally launched the Reformation in 1517 by nailing a sheet of paper to the door of a church in the city of Wittenberg, the last barriers to chaos gave way. The result was more than a century of brutal religious warfare.

Taborite ideas played a significant role in the opening phases of the violence. In the decades before the outbreak of the Reformation, news from Bohemia had traveled far and wide, and inspired a series of German peasant risings against the Church and the nobility—at Niklashausen in 1474, and in Speyer in 1502, 1513, and 1517—all of which drew heavily on imagery from the Book of Revelation and from Taborite propaganda as well. In 1520, a priest named Thomas Müntzer was caught up in this same current of ideas, and became convinced that the millennial kingdom would arise just as soon as the righteous carried out a campaign of extermination against all the foes of God.

It took Müntzer five years to find a receptive audience. During that time he wandered through central Europe, preaching his gospel of salvation through mass murder and publishing a series of lurid pamphlets denouncing all those who disagreed with him as slaves of the Antichrist. In 1525, though, peasants across much of Germany rose in revolt against their overlords, and Müntzer quickly found himself with a following. After several months of inconclusive raids and skirmishes, the peasants' army and a strong force of nobles and mercenaries headed by Philip, Landgrave of Hesse, faced each other on May 15.

Müntzer urged his forces on to battle, insisting that God had revealed to him that their enemies would be slaughtered and that he himself would catch the nobles' cannon-shot in the sleeves of his coat. The sudden appearance of a rainbow in the sky was cheered by the peasants as an additional sign from God of their approaching victory. It so happened that the nobles chose that moment to open fire with their cannon, mowing down many of the peasants and putting the others to flight. Müntzer managed to escape the battlefield but was caught hiding in a cellar a few days later, and was tortured and beheaded by the victors.

The sorry ending of the Peasants' War, as the 1525 revolt

came to be called, did little to discourage further attempts to bring paradise at gunpoint. No sooner was the revolt over than a disciple of Müntzer's named Hans Hut began to proclaim that the Second Coming would take place in 1528, and would be followed by the usual slaughter of nobles and priests. Hut was captured in 1527 and died in prison that year, but followers of his tried to organize a revolt the following year in southwest Germany. They got nowhere; still, their ideas spread rapidly and helped set off an explosion a few years later in the town of Münster far to the north in Holland.

Like many European cities in those days, Münster was ruled officially by the local Catholic bishop and unofficially by the heads of the town's merchant guilds, and the division of power between the two was a source of constant turmoil and occasional open combat. In 1533 the guilds gained the upper hand, drove out the bishop, and installed Lutheran ministers in all the town churches as a further declaration of their independence. In the process, they welcomed other religious dissidents into Münster, including the radical preacher Jan Matthys. Matthys was a brilliant rabble-rouser, and he quickly won the support of a large faction of the population; in 1534 Matthys took control of the town, expelled the minority of dissidents, and set out to turn Münster into the New Jerusalem predicted in the Book of Revelation.

The bishop of Münster by this time was back with an army, and laid siege to the town. Matthys and his followers fought back energetically. On Easter Sunday of 1534, convinced that God would grant him victory and usher in the millennium on the spot, Matthys led an assault on the besiegers with a small party of followers. God apparently had other plans, and Matthys and all those who went with him were hacked to pieces by the bishop's forces. Matthys' disciple Jan Bockelson quickly took charge of the city, and proceeded to proclaim himself the Messiah.

Bockelson's idea of a messianic kingdom drew heavily on some two thousand years of Jewish and Christian imagery, filtered through the mind of a would-be intellectual with little education and a spectacular case of megalomania. As King of the New Jerusalem, he revived the Old Testament custom of polygamy, amassing a harem of fifteen wives; he organized a court of some two hundred officers who lived in luxury while the rest of the population of Münster struggled to stay fed and clothed. His agents slipped out through enemy lines and attempted to set off revolts in other cities, with some success—a rising in the province of Groningen, led by a man who called himself Christ, the Son of God, marched toward Münster until they were defeated and scattered by the Duke of Gelderland; revolts also broke out in Minden and Amsterdam and were put down only after heavy fighting.

It was not until June 24, 1535, that Bockelson's reign finally ended. That night, helped by deserters from within the walls, a surprise attack by the bishop's troops and allies broke into the city, and after several hours of desperate fighting the New Jerusalem fell. Most of the rebels were massacred on the spot; Bockelson and two other leaders were led away in chains, and in January of 1536 they were tortured to death with red-hot irons. According to all accounts, Bockelson remained dignified and silent during the entire process of his agonizing death.

Ω

The Peasants' War and the Münster rebellion belonged to the first phase of the Reformation, when religious violence was mostly the result of local wars and apocalyptic revolts. Thereafter, things spun out of control on a broader scale. Not long after Bockelson's death, the religious struggle between Protestants and Catholics in France began to turn violent, ending in a bitter civil war that occupied much of the second half of the century. In 1618, the wary truce between Protestant and Catholic provinces in Germany finally collapsed into the carnage of the Thirty Years War, and in 1640, England wrapped up its own complicated trajectory through the religious disputes of the time with a civil war of its own, which pitted conservative Episcopalians gathered around the King against radical Puritans who supported the cause of Parliament. By the time the fighting finally drew to an end, France had passed through a brief period of religious liberty and then returned to the Catholic fold; England had executed a king, experimented with a Puritan dictatorship, and reestablished a Protestant monarchy; Holland had survived a bitter war of independence; Germany had been ravaged from end to end by vast armies; and the countries that had managed to keep the fighting outside their borders—Catholic Italy, Spain, and

Poland on the one hand, and Protestant Scandinavia on the other—were shaking their collective heads at the scale of the slaughter.

In the wake of the Wars of Religion, it started to sink in across much of Europe that there might be something amiss with ways of thinking that promised one glorious redemption after another, but succeeded mostly in bringing about unparalleled destruction. As the surviving powers took stock of the wreckage, a sustained opposition to the apocalypse meme began to take shape. A great many thinkers in the two centuries or so after the Peace of Westphalia in 1648 remembered all too well the havoc that the apocalypse meme had helped unleash, and began to challenge the idea that the lavish imagery of the Book of Revelation ought to be used to interpret contemporary political and religious struggles.

It's one of the great ironies of history that the shift away from a politics of religious apocalyptic turned out to provide a major boost to the apocalypse meme itself. Cut loose from the world of theology, it found plenty of new fodder in the realms of nationalist politics, social agitation, and racial and ethnic hatred. Within a few centuries of the Peace of Westphalia, as a result, secular versions of the apocalypse meme would cause bloodshed on a scale vastly greater than anything brought about by the sixteenth- and seventeenth-century wars of religion.

CHAPTER FOUR:

THE WANING OF THEOLOGY

The first secular forms of the apocalypse meme actually began to take shape well back in the Middle Ages, with the earliest stirrings of what radicals of a later age would call "class consciousness." The Peasants' Revolt that erupted in England in 1381, while it drew on some of the traditional rhetoric of religious apocalyptic, already displayed themes that would be central to the secular apocalyptic to come. When the rural poor who marched to London with Wat Tyler and John Ball chanted "When Adam delved and Eve span, who was then the gentleman?" they provided the aristocracy of their time with an unwelcome preview of the Bastille and the Winter Palace. Similar themes appeared in other peasant risings, including those in Reformation Germany discussed in Chapter Three; the admixture of religious imagery varied, but the common theme—that paradise could be gained by eliminating social hierarchies, and usually everyone in the upper levels of those hierarchies as well—was common to all.

Even further back, a curious nationalist offshoot of religious apocalyptic provided an eerie foreshadowing of the nationalist wars of a later time. Across much of the medieval world, the belief emerged that some famous and long-dead hero was not dead at all, but would reappear in glory sometime in the future and lead his people to triumph over their national enemies. In the Celtic lands of Wales, Cornwall, and Brittany, the figure in question was King Arthur; in Germany, it was the Holy Roman Emperor Frederick I; in Hungary, it was Attila the Hun, from whose hordes the Hungarians in those days claimed descent, and so on. Weirdly, the same notion appeared at the same time on the far side of the Atlantic: in the wake of the fall of the Toltec Empire, people across medieval Mexico believed that the great Toltec king Quetzalcoatl had not died after all, but sailed east over the sea on a raft of snakes and would reappear some day. That belief, as it turned out, played a significant role in leaving the Aztec Empire wide open to the Spanish conquistadors under Hernan Cortes.

This same set of beliefs also came to play a profoundly important role in shaping the history of the Muslim world as well. After the death of Muhammad, the prophet of Islam, a schism emerged among his followers. Some accepted the leadership of Abu Bakr, the prophet's father-in-law; others supported the claims of his son-in-law 'Ali and the bloodline descended from him and Fatimah, the prophet's only living child. The former party became the Sunni, the followers of the *sunnah* or consensus of tradition; the latter became the Shi'a, a contraction of *shiat 'Ali*, "supporters of 'Ali," who considered the male successors of 'Ali to be divinely inspired prophets.

According to the most widely accepted version of Shi'a teaching, there were twelve of these successors, or imams. The last of them, a five-year-old boy, disappeared in 870 during a fierce persecution of the Shi'a community by the dominant Sunni sect. In the wake of his disappearance, however, Shi'ite Muslims insisted that the Twelfth Imam was not dead but in hiding, concealed by Allah from a hostile world, and that he would continue to be the hidden guide and teacher of all Shi'ites until the end of the world, when he and Jesus would reappear and overcome the forces of evil. This remains the most popular version of Shi'ite doctrine today, and Shi'ite mystics from the Middle Ages to the present day have reported visionary encounters with the Hidden Imam and his companions.

Even where the belief in a "Once and Future King" did not take on as overtly a religious dimension as it did in the Muslim world, the hidden or sleeping monarch who would return some day became a potent political force. The hope of King Arthur's return became a theme used by generations of fighters for Welsh and Breton independence, while Frederick II's public relations people tried, not without success, to cash in on the belief in the earlier Frederick's eventual return. Still, the main current of secular apocalypticism took a different direction. Before the Wars of Religion had finished winding down, the radicalism that had been given voice in the Peasants' Revolt had found its voice as the core theme of the new prophecies of history's end.

Ω

The first clear snapshot of the new apocalypticism surfaced in England, in the wake of the English Civil War of 1641–1645. For many English radicals, the defeat of King Charles and his aristocratic supporters by the thoroughly proletarian Roundheads seemed to promise nothing less than the imminent arrival of paradise on Earth, and the collapse of government censorship in the wake of the royalist defeat allowed a dizzying number of viewpoints to find their way into the thriving print media of the time. Churned out by the wagonload by hand-operated printing presses across England, books, pamphlets, and broadsheets announcing the approaching dawn of a new world found readers across the country, and sparked disputes as loud and intransigent as any of today's Internet flamewars.

There were, to be sure, plenty of people who invoked the traditional rhetoric of Christian apocalypticism. The Fifth Monarchy Men, a significant movement of the time, took their name from their belief that the English kingship had been the last of the four monarchies prophesied in the Book of Daniel, and a fifth monarchy—the personal rule of Jesus—could be expected to begin any day now. The delightfully named Muggletonians, along the same lines, drew their inspiration from the prophet Lodowicke Muggleton. Muggleton believed that he and his cousin John Reeve were the two witnesses predicted in the Book of Revelation, whose appearance marked the imminence of the Second Coming. There were plenty of others—enough of them that most observers simply lumped them together under their most obvious common characteristic, and called them Ranters.

Still, one of the most famous radical groups of the time— the Diggers—took a different approach. Their chief theoretician, Gerrard Winstanley, began to announce in 1649 that the old world was wearing away and a new world of perfect equality was about to dawn. He and his followers founded a commune near Cobham in Surrey, where all property was held in common and what labor got done was shared equally among the members. Winstanley's lively writings include the argument that all wealth was simply an expression of human labor; this labor theory of value would later be developed in much more detail, by another apocalyptic prophet whose work, covered later in this chapter, would have a far larger impact.

Winstanley's commune inspired a flurry of imitators and sparked an even larger flurry of criticism in the media of the time. His calls for the abolition of private property caused no small panic in the English middle classes of the time, and it didn't help matters that other figures at the same time were calling for such unthinkably radical measures as giving women the right to vote. Thus the early 1650s saw a backlash against the radicals. Spearheaded by Oliver Cromwell, who made an easy transition from commander of the Roundhead armies to military dictator of Great Britain, backed by plenty of ordinary Britons who were scared out of their wits by the radicals, and eventually fixed into place by the restoration of King Charles' son to a strictly limited monarchy, the new conservatism failed to eliminate the Ranters, Diggers, Muggletonians, and their peers, but succeeded in driving them to the fringes of British society.

There they remained, and to a very real extent, there they still remain. There were active Muggletonian groups in Britain well into the eighteenth century. As the eighteenth century gave way to the nineteenth, in turn, the British fringe was enlivened by the activities of such figures as Richard Brothers and Joanna Southcott. Brothers proclaimed himself God's nephew, declared that the English were descended from the lost tribes of Israel, and proposed to lead them home to Palestine in a mass migration. Southcott, a West Country folk healer and fortune-teller turned prophetess, became the center of a lively movement with congregations across much of England, and at age sixty-five announced that she was pregnant with the Messiah. Instead of giving birth, however, she died, and her followers kept her body warm with hot-water bottles, hoping for a resurrection, until the smell became intolerable.

Ω

Long before Brothers and Southcott had their time in the spotlight, though, the center of secular apocalyptic in the Western world had leapt the English Channel and found a new and welcoming home in France. There the same sort of over-the-top absolutism that cost England's King Charles I his head had not yet encountered a limiting factor on the scale of Cromwell and his Roundhead army, and flourished to the point of absurdity, by turns encouraged and undercut by a large and greedy aristocracy and a national church far more obviously interested in worldly wealth and influence than in saving souls. The sheer improbability of meaningful reform in the face of these entrenched powers inspired a great many French intellectuals to dream of a perfect society that would arrive all at once if only the existing order of things could somehow be overthrown.

These Utopian dreams drew on one or both of two broad currents of thought. The first of these was rationalism, the belief that a perfect world could be brought about by discarding the heritage of the past and rebuilding all human affairs on the basis of pure logic. By the early decades of the eighteenth century, ideas of this kind had begun to win support across a broad sector of France's middle classes and even found an audience here and there in the aristocracy itself. In 1750, when a group of scholars headed by Denis Diderot and Jean Le Rond d'Alembert announced the forthcoming production of the first modern encyclopedia, the rationalist movement found a banner around which to gather.

The Encyclopédie, published in fifteen volumes between 1751 and 1765, subjected the traditional ideals and customs at the foundation of French society to scathing critique. In the oppressive political climate of the time, this had predictable results. Diderot and many of his coauthors spent time in prison repeatedly during the production of the Encyclopédie, and publication was suspended several times by the royal censors, but the resulting furor sent sales skyrocketing and made the Encyclopédistes heroes to all those—and there were many of them in France and elsewhere—who found the fossilized social order of eighteenth-century Europe increasingly hard to tolerate.

The second current that shaped the secular apocalypticism of the time was primitivism, the belief that a perfect world could be brought into being by discarding everything that was false, artificial, and unnatural, and allowing humanity to return to a presumably natural state of peace and harmony. The major figure in the primitivist movement in eighteenth-century France was the Swiss philosopher Jean-Jacques Rousseau, who spent most of his life in France and whose wildly popular writings—*On the Origins of Inequality, The Social Contract,* and others—asked all the hard questions about the origins and logic of a social system that gave unearned wealth to a few and condemned everyone else to pay the price. Rousseau's primitivism cohabited uneasily at best with the rationalist current that dominated the cultural conversation of the time; Rousseau himself was briefly allied with Diderot and the other Encyclopédistes, and wrote several important articles for the Encyclopédie, before a series of pyrotechnic quarrels sent him spinning off on an orbit of his own. Like Diderot, he was rarely out of trouble with the French government for long.

What no one seems to have noticed at the time, or for many years thereafter, was the dependence of both these currents of thought on the old religious apocalyptic that Rousseau and the Encyclopédistes alike rejected with so much scorn. The rationalist notion of a perfect society about to dawn once pure reason governed human affairs drew much of its imagery and no small amount of its force from Joachim of Flores' prophecy of an imminent Age of Liberty in which heaven would be realized right here on Earth. Rousseau's primitivism, with its fond backward glance at a golden age of simplicity when human beings had lived in pastoral harmony with all creation, drew just as deeply from Christian tradition by rewriting the story of Eden in secular terms, with the invention of private property filling the place of the apple.

In this way, the apocalypse meme found a new home in the world of radical ideology. Well before the end of the eighteenth century, the first fully developed secular apocalyptic took shape beneath the busy pen of Nicolas de Caritat, marquis de Condorcet. Condorcet was a rationalist of the first order, a brilliant mathematician and an advocate for the abolition of slavery and equal rights for women. In 1784, he completed what many people consider to be his greatest work, *Sketch for a Historical Picture of the Progress of the Human Mind*, which redefined history as a process of mental and political emancipation that would inevitably lead humanity to a Utopian world of never-ending improvement.

Condorcet's prophecy was all the more remarkable in that he wrote the *Sketch* while in hiding from the secret police of France's Revolutionary government. Shortly after completing it, he was located, arrested, and thrown in prison, where he died. The great overturning of the established order of France had arrived at last, but the result was neither a great leap forward to a society of reason and light nor a return to the pastoral Eden of natural human goodness imagined by Rousseau. Instead, radical parties struggled for power over a system just as dictatorial as the one they had overthrown, and sent their opponents in cartloads to the guillotine. The political chaos and the killings did not subside until an ambitious artillery officer named Napoleon Bonaparte staged a coup, seized power, suppressed the revolutionary ideologies that had given him his window of opportunity, and launched France into a series of catastrophic wars that ravaged Europe for a quarter century.

After the Napoleonic Wars finally ended in the mass carnage of the Battle of Waterloo, and Napoleon himself was packed off on a British warship to spend the rest of his days in exile on the barren volcanic island of St. Helena half a world away from France, the great powers of the day met at Vienna and tried to accomplish the same thing their predecessors had done in crafting the Peace of Westphalia. Meanwhile, just as the Wars of Religion had sparked a backlash against religious apocalypticism, the French Revolution and the Napoleonic Wars that followed it inspired an equivalent backlash against the secular form.

Much of this backlash took the shape given it by one

man, the Anglo-Irish writer and statesman Edmund Burke. Active in what we would now consider liberal political causes for most of his adult life, and a strong supporter of the rights of the American colonists in the years leading up to the American Revolution, Burke was perceptive enough even in extreme old age to recognize that what drove the French Revolution was something different. His last book, *Reflections on the Revolution in France* (1790), outlined with fine clarity the difference between improving a system through thoughtful reform, and tearing it down under the unthinking assumption that whatever took its place must, by definition, be an improvement. Once the fighting was over and the cost of France's apocalyptic enthusiasm became clear, Burke's ideas became hugely influential. For most of the two centuries that followed, the more thoughtful and principled end of the conservative movement across the Western world embraced Burke's vision in theory, though they often enough fell short of it in practice.

Still, the hard turn away from apocalyptic that followed the end of the Wars of Religion was not repeated in the wake of the Congress of Vienna, and all the eloquence of Burke and his successors could not change that. The cat was well and truly out of the bag; the idea that Utopia could be obtained by the simple expedient of violent revolution was far too tempting a bait, and the great powers that defeated Napoleon compounded the problem by trying to impose a rigidly conservative pattern on restive nationalities across Europe. The apocalyptic notions that took shape in France before the Revolution thus spread rapidly across the continent, sparking repeated attempts at revolt and laying the groundwork for the most catastrophically successful secular apocalyptic movement of all time.

Ω

During the years that religious versions of the apocalypse meme were losing popularity in Europe, however, they found eager listeners elsewhere in the world. The spread of European empires around the globe during the age of exploration placed traditional societies everywhere under overwhelming pressure, while the Christian missionaries who normally accompanied imperial adventures carried the apocalypse meme with them as part of their intellectual baggage. It took very little time for indigenous people to pry the meme loose from its Christian setting and reframe it in terms drawn from their own traditions, and the temptation to do so in the face of European inroads was far too great for many societies to resist.

The Tupi-Guarani people of the Amazon rain forest provide one example out of many. Like many of the First Nations of the Amazon basin, the Tupi-Guarani believe that the universe was established by the Creator on two crossed bars; these bars mark the Sun's positions at the solstices and equinoxes, the frame of the cosmos according to the archaic star wisdom explored back in Chapter One. When the crossed bars eventually slip, and the Tupi-Guarani believe that someday they inevitably will, the world will be destroyed by fire as it was once in the past destroyed by flood.

At the time of the last destruction, according to legend, the culture heroes of the Tupi-Guarani escaped the waters by purifying themselves and traveling to the Land Without Evil, which lies somewhere far to the east beyond a great river. From ancient times, accordingly, groups of Tupi-Guarani inspired by the visions of native prophets have set out in search of the Land Without Evil, and much of the historic distribution of the Tupi-Guarani people in Brazil is a result of migrations that this process set in motion.

Still, the arrival of European ideas—backed up inevitably by European firearms—transformed this tradition, turning it into more fodder for the apocalypse meme. Beginning not long after the European conquest of the Amazon basin, and continuing well into the twentieth century, a succession of Tupi-Guarani prophets have claimed that the crossed bars that support the world were slipping, the destruction by fire was imminent, and only those who escaped to the Land Without Evil would be saved. Mass movements of Tupi-Guarani have responded by surging across the landscape in any direction that promised to lead them toward the Land Without Evil—which in most cases was also away from the political and economic control of the European-descended ruling classes. Some of those journeys ended in tragedy; others simply kept going until geographical or political barriers forced them to stop; none of them reached the Land Without Evil, but that did nothing to keep each subsequent generation from trying again.

The impact of apocalyptic ideas from Europe on the rest of the world became even more intense, and more global, as the nineteenth century began and European powers learned how to turn the power of steam engines and modern weaponry into tools for building empires. Backed by expansionist political agendas and the firepower of the new weapons, millions of European settlers headed out to seize lands occupied by other peoples. Where the technological gap was wide enough, as in North America and Australia, and temperate climates suited European modes of settlement, the indigenous peoples were driven off their lands onto barren reservations, or simply massacred. Some of the most desperate of all history's apocalyptic movements rose up in response—perhaps the most tragic example of all was the Ghost Dance movement among the First Nations of the plains states of North America.

The Ghost Dance had plenty of antecedents. Beginning in the seventeenth century, Christian missionaries among the native tribes of North America spread a distinctively Protestant form of the apocalypse meme that focused on repentance and contrition as the triggers that would bring the long-awaited end of the world. These ideas blended easily with native traditions in which purification and ascetic practices opened the way to visionary experiences of the spirit world, and gave rise to hybrid movements in which a native prophet would call on his people to reject the trappings of European culture and purify themselves with sacred dances and songs, so that spirit powers would drive back the invaders and bring a new and better world.

Wovoka, the Paiute visionary whose visions launched the Ghost Dance movement on its way, was a prophet of this kind. During a solar eclipse on January 1, 1889, he had a vision of a world of perfect peace and plenty, which would surely arrive if all the native peoples of the Western plains purified themselves and performed a sacred dance. The plains tribes, which had been driven off their ancestral lands and were facing starvation as a result of the extermination of the buffalo herds, were ready to hear such a message, and tribe after tribe took up the Ghost Dance. Somewhere along the way, the movement picked up a militant dimension absent from Wovoka's original vision. By the time they reached the Lakota Nation of the northern plains, the Ghost Dance teachings included the belief that the coming of the new world would involve the mass extermination of the white invaders, and the belief that "ghost shirts" made in a sacred manner would repel bullets.

The Lakota had been a thorn in the side of the US government's expansionist agenda for decades, and the arrival of the new movement at a time when many Lakota were on the edge of starvation convinced US Army officials on the scene that another war between the Lakota and the United States might be in the offing. More troops and weapons were sent for, and regulations banning the Ghost Dance issued. A flashpoint was probably inevitable; when it arrived, at Wounded Knee on December 28, 1890, US soldiers opened fire with field artillery and Hotchkiss machine guns on a mostly unarmed band of Lakota Ghost Dancers. Most of the 153 killed were women or children. Twenty soldiers received the Congressional Medal of Honor for their roles in the slaughter.

Ω

The same pattern of fusion that combined the apocalypse meme with long-established local traditions also took place in societies where the technological gap was much narrower. China, which had been one of the world's great powers until European empires equipped themselves with the tools of modern warfare, is a case in point. As discussed back in Chapter One, China has had its own distinctive model of violent apocalyptic rebellion since ancient times, but that model was always open to good ideas from overseas, and the missionary Christianity of the age of European expansion provided a bumper crop of raw material for yet another round of insurgency against the imperial government. There had been a steady drumbeat of small-scale uprisings by sects of the Yellow Turban variety all along, but by the middle years of the nineteenth century, as the Yuan Dynasty tottered under rising pressure from Europe's colonial powers, the time was right for something bigger and more up-to-date.

It arrived at the hands of Hong Xiuquan, a child of Hakka farmers in Guangdong province in the south of China, one of countless upwardly mobile young men of his time whose hopes for the future centered on passing the imperial civil service examination and entering a career as a government official. He passed the initial qualifying examination, but failed repeatedly to pass the main examination. He returned home, fell sick, and took to his bed, convinced he was about to die.

Instead, he had a series of visions that convinced him that he was none other than the second son of the Christian god, Jesus's younger brother, who was destined to drive demons out of heaven and earth and inaugurate the heavenly kingdom throughout the world, beginning with China. He recovered from his illness and began to preach; converts came slowly at first, but after a few years he had gained the loyalty of several passionate and effective preachers, and his following began to grow rapidly. Borrowing the traditional phrase, he called his movement the Taiping Tianguo, the Heavenly Kingdom of Great Peace.

The peace of the Heavenly Kingdom, however, had sharp edges. As the movement grew, Hong organized military units and used them to suppress the bandits and pirates who infested southern China at that time. This movement toward militancy alarmed the imperial government, which began to persecute the sect; Hong responded in 1850 by proclaiming himself Heavenly King and declaring war against the empire. Units of the imperial army sent to suppress the rising were driven off with heavy casualties. Before long Hong was the absolute ruler of most of four provinces and could field an army as strong as anything the Chinese government was able to bring against him.

It took twelve years for the imperial government, with substantial help from the major European powers of the time, to overcome the Heavenly Kingdom. Both sides quickly adopted policies of total warfare, destroying crops and infrastructure in an effort to weaken the other side's ability to carry on the fight. All told, something like twenty million people died in what was one of the nineteenth century's largest and most savage wars.

Among the Europeans who helped the Chinese government crush the Taiping Rebellion was Charles Gordon, a British army officer who was placed in command of a Chinese force, the Ever-Victorious Army, and led it to a series of notable victories that won him high honors from both the British and Chinese governments. After several successful postings elsewhere in the world, he was sent to Sudan. His mission was to deal with yet another apocalyptic rebellion.

This time he was not so fortunate. The Sudanese uprising was led by Muhammad Ahmad, a charismatic religious leader who had proclaimed himself the Mahdi—the figure who, in Muslim thought, is to appear at the end of time and usher in the millennial kingdom—and who succeeded in uniting most of the Sudanese people under his leadership. Within a month of Gordon's arrival in the Sudanese capital at Khartoum, in February of 1884, the city was surrounded by the Mahdi's forces, and a siege began. A British relief force headed down the Nile to rescue Gordon, but two days before it reached Khartoum, the rebel forces broke into the city and Gordon and his troops were killed. The relief expedition was forced back to Egypt, and Sudan remained independent until 1898, when a heavily armed British expedition fought its way up the Nile and reconquered the country.

Ω

The inhabitants of the lands faced with Europe's explosive colonial expansion were not the only peoples to face drastic cultural change as the nineteenth century drew on. The new industrial order of society had an equally large impact on European cultures, though that impact generally drew secular rather than religious responses, and a great many of those responses drew inspiration from the same French rationalist and primitivist radical ideas that helped to launch the Napoleonic Wars. As soon as Napoleon's empire had been crushed, in fact, the ideas his government and his opponents had both done their best to suppress came surging up out of the crawlspaces of European society in a series of attempted revolts that, at one time or another, affected most of the countries of Europe.

The shadowy presence behind these risings was the Carbonari, a name that haunted the nightmares of conservatives for three generations until Karl Marx gave them something more serious to worry about. The Carbonari started out as an ordinary fraternal society organized along Masonic lines, with its own passwords and secret handshakes, and an origin legend involving poor but honest Scottish charcoal burners and a king of France who, according to the story, managed to get lost while hunting along the nonexistent border between France and Scotland. In the hothouse environment of French-ruled Italy, rebels against Napoleon's empire found such things useful; they took over the old society and turned it into an effective framework for revolutionary conspiracy.

After Napoleon's fall, Carbonaros spread across Europe, forming local lodges wherever they went, recruiting disaffected intellectuals and members of the middle classes, and instructing each newly initiated member to buy a rifle, fifty cartridges, and a dagger, for use when the revolution began. The revolutions duly began: in Italy and Spain in 1820, Greece in 1821, Russia in 1824, France in 1830, Italy again in 1831, and across most of Europe in 1848. Nearly all of these failed, but the threat of a Carbonaro rising kept the heat under reactionary governments across Europe, and drove them to grant a range of freedoms to their people in the hopes of forestalling yet another attempted revolution.

By and large, the Carbonari steered clear of apocalyptic fantasies in the strict sense; the closest they came was the normal revolutionary fantasy that Utopia could be obtained by throwing the current set of scoundrels out of power and putting a new set in their place. Here and there in the movement, though, radical thinkers were beginning to piece together ideologies that set their sights higher. Filippo Buonarroti, one of the most influential organizers of the post-Napoleonic revolutionary scheme, was one of these. He sketched out in his pamphlets and speeches a vision of the future in which the violent annihilation of all existing governments would lead to a future in which everyone would live in perfect equality and peace. As the nineteenth century proceeded, such ideas gained support from an astonishingly unlikely source.

Charles Fourier was a traveling salesman who lived, between journeys, in the French town of Lyons. Born in

1772, he managed to steer clear of the revolutionary enthu-
siasms that kept the majority of his countrymen fighting
each other and much of the rest of Europe through most of
his adult life. Instead, he devoted his time to elaborating, in
vast detail, one of the most engagingly dotty ideologies in
the history of human thought.

Readers who scent an overstatement in this last description clearly haven't encountered Fourierism. Fourier argued
that passional attraction was the supreme force of the cosmos.
Under its power, worlds coalesced out of the "interstellar
aroma" and cycled through a predetermined history in
which the discovery of Fourier's own philosophy, endlessly
repeated on countless worlds, was always the crucial turning
point. Humanity on this world, like every other, progressed
step-by-step through the stages of Savagery, Barbarism, and
Civilization, before finally reaching the culminating state
of Harmony—that is, Fourierism.

Exactly what would happen once Harmony was attained
on Earth was, like almost everything else imaginable, spelled
out in vast and lurid detail in the pages of Fourier's voluminous writings. As soon as a single small community embraced
the Harmonial Philosophy, Fourier insisted, torrents of
"cosmic citric acid" would descend from the heavens
and turn the seas to lemonade; four stray moons that had
circled Earth during the planet's infancy would come home
from their wanderings and grace the skies; warm auroras
would turn the barren lands around both poles into green
and inviting agricultural regions, and lions would give up
their carnivorous habits and become friendly, vegetarian

anti-lions. Passional attraction would solve all social problems, and human beings would settle down to a long and
lively future spent mostly in gourmet dining ("gastrosophy")
and orgiastic sex, interspersed with brief periods of leisurely
work at frequently changing tasks which, being motivated
by passional attraction, would produce unimaginable material abundance.

Fourier's first book, *Théorie des quatre mouvements* (*Theory
of the Four Movements*), originally saw print in 1809. Most
of Europe was worrying about other things just then—the
Napoleonic Wars, for example—and so it took a while for
the prophet of Harmony to find an audience for his vision.
The end of the fighting, however, brought Fourier the first
of a steady stream of followers, and by the time of his death
in 1837 he and his ideas had become famous throughout
Europe and in North America as well. Lured, perhaps, by
the promise of lemonade oceans and cuddlesome anti-lions,
dozens of groups on both continents launched Fourierist
communes, though none of them lasted for more than a
couple of years—expecting people to work only when
they felt the urgings of passional attraction, it turned out,
meant that nobody did enough work to keep a community
running, much less pay the bills—and the promised millennium failed to arrive.

Despite these repeated failures and the extravagant weird-
ness of Fourier's philosophy, some of the ideas he put into
circulation spread widely, and encouraged thinkers to offer
somewhat less giddy social theories of their own. One of the
many terms Fourier coined in the process of expounding his

theories, for example, was the word "feminist." Even more influential in the years that followed his death was a concept that he never got around to naming, but that formed one of the foundations of his economic thought: the theory that the means of economic production should be owned by the community rather than by individuals. The theorists of a later generation, who borrowed this concept from Fourier, called it "socialism."

Ω

It's almost impossible to imagine two figures in the history of human thought who were less alike than Charles Fourier and the next major name in the development of secular apocalypticism, Georg Wilhelm Friedrich Hegel. Very nearly the only things they had in common were that they both wrote huge and mostly unreadable books, and they both considered themselves and their ideas to be of vast world-historical importance. Those two habits, to be sure, were shared by plenty of intellectuals in their time. Rarely have so many obscure philosophers, novelists, poets, and political theorists been so ready to imagine their work as history's supreme turning point, and it's one of history's jests that rarely have so many of its great turning points fallen so deeply into well-earned oblivion.

Some of the core differences between the two men unfolded from their very different social positions. Where Fourier was an outsider to the scholarly world of his time, Hegel was a consummate insider, working his way up the ladder of a standard nineteenth-century German academic career from private lecturer at the University of Jena, editor of a literary newspaper in Bamberg, headmaster of a high school in Nuremberg, professor at the University of Heidelberg, and finally the chair of philosophy at the University of Berlin, which he occupied until his death. His publications followed the same careful, professional route, from an utterly unmemorable doctoral dissertation to his first major work, *The Phenomenology of Spirit*, which staked his claim to one particular version of nineteenth-century idealist philosophy, and then to a series of progressively longer and more ambitious works applying the same ideas to various fashionable fields of thought.

History was one of those fields. In Hegel's study of history, if it's possible to sum up so great a body of convoluted reasoning and impenetrable prose in a few short sentences, he argued that history is the process by which the Absolute gradually manifests itself in the world of space and time. The manifestation of the Absolute unfolds in a sequence by which each state of being generates conflicts due to its own internal contradictions, and these result in a struggle by which the contradictions are resolved in a new synthesis; the synthesis then reveals its own internal contradictions, and the process goes on from there.

It doesn't go on forever, though, for eventually the Absolute will have completely manifested itself in space and time, at which point history will stop and a perfect human society will have been achieved. The emergence of a world-historical personality who would embody the

Absolute, Hegel suggested, would play a central role in this final transformation. Hegel himself waffled about when this would happen, though toward the end of his career, comfortably settled in Berlin and well aware where his personal advantage lay, he argued that the perfect society had in fact been achieved in late nineteenth-century Germany.

Attentive readers may already have noticed the similarities between this set of ideas and those of Joachim of Flores; these parallels are anything but accidental. Hegel, in fact, could be considered the nineteenth century's supreme Joachimist. Though Hegel apparently never discussed his twelfth-century predecessor in print and may never have read Joachim's works directly, the ideas of the Italian mystic run barefoot through the writings of the German pedant. It's not just that the Absolute is Hegel's demure nineteenth-century idealist way of talking about Joachim's God, or that the stages of his version of history bear more than a little family resemblance to the ages of Law, Grace, and Freedom as Joachim expounded them; the most important similarity is that the redefinition of history as the grand unfolding of a spiritual agenda over the centuries was central to both men's work. That the hurly-burly of events that made up humanity's experience had to have a purpose and a goal— that was the heart of Hegel's teaching, as it was of Joachim's, and it proved just as irresistible to the intellectuals of the nineteenth and twentieth centuries as it had to those of the thirteenth and fourteenth.

One of those nineteenth-century intellectuals was a serious young man named Karl Marx. Born in a Jewish family that converted to Lutheranism when he was a young boy, Marx attended university in Bonn and Berlin. Hegel had been dead for only five years when Marx came to Berlin to study, and the younger man soon became part of a circle of radical Hegelians who were reshaping the old philosopher's theories in political directions. After receiving his doctorate in 1841, Marx spent a short time working for a radical newspaper in Cologne; the paper was soon shut down by the authorities, and Marx moved to Paris, where he found another post as a journalist and spent his off-hours in the thriving subculture of left-wing politics that made Paris the center of European radicalism. He spent the next few years being thrown out of one European country after another for political agitation, before finally settling in England and devoting most of his time to writing. The first volume of his magnum opus, *Capital*, was published in 1867; the two remaining volumes were finished by his close friend Friedrich Engels and published after Marx's death in 1883.

As an economist and a social philosopher, Marx remains a towering figure. Even those who reject his ideas most forcefully have had to address his arguments in detail, and his critical analysis of capitalist economics, despite some serious flaws, deserves close reading even today. These are not the elements of his work that ended up dominating the history of the twentieth century, though. From Hegel, Marx took the idea of history as a series of stages which succeed one another as the internal contradictions of each one give rise to a new synthesis, and the broader sense of history as a linear process moving inexorably toward a goal. The great innovation of Marx's version of history was that he eliminated the religious and idealistic dimensions of Hegel's thought and brought it firmly down to the plane of politics and economics.

The result was an extraordinarily powerful version of the apocalypse meme for a secular age. Marx argued that the world was moving step-by-step toward a transformation nearly as total as anything Zarathustra predicted, but the forces driving the process were political and economic rather than supernatural, and the millennium would be brought about by violent revolution rather than by divine intervention. The capitalist system, he predicted, would inevitably become more and more oppressive and burdensome over time, until, finally, the working classes, driven to the edge of starvation, would rise up, slaughter their capitalist masters, and usher in a new socialist society governed by a dictatorship of the working class, which would in turn naturally give way to the Utopian state of communism at some point in the future. Under capitalism, the means of economic production were owned by individuals and workers were exploited ruthlessly; under socialism, the means of economic production would be owned by the state and workers would get a fair share of the profits of their labors; under communism, the state would wither away, the workers would own the means of production directly, and everyone would contribute equally to production and share equally in the world's wealth.

In the grim industrial slums of late nineteenth- and early twentieth century Europe, this was heady brew, and it soon won a devout following throughout the industrial world. By the beginning of the twentieth century, as a result, there were large Marxist parties in every industrial nation that allowed political parties at all. Observers at the time noted with some discomfort that these parties had more than a passing resemblance to churches, complete with fierce debates about the fine points of dogma. Still, there had been plenty of radical political movements all through the nineteenth century, and the governments of Europe had been able to keep them at bay through various combinations of widely ballyhooed reforms and massive police brutality. Very few people thought that the new Marxist radical movements would pose a more serious challenge than the Carbonari.

Equally, though, very few people expected the great powers of Europe to blunder into one of history's most devastating wars in the summer of 1914. A great many crystal balls apparently stopped working right about that time; British generals who blithely promised that the troops would be home by Christmas and German field marshals who expected to drive straight across France to the sea found themselves trapped in an utterly unexpected stalemate, in which the same few square miles of blood-soaked mud might change hands ten times in a year, at the cost of tens of thousands of deaths for each exchange.

Before long, it became agonizingly clear that the bloodshed would go on until the warring nations started to collapse, and the only question was who would collapse first. In March of 1917, that question was settled when the Russian Empire imploded. By October of that year the

Communist party, under the leadership of Vladimir I. Lenin, had seized power. The civil war that followed left the Communists firmly in charge, and when Germany turned out to be the next country to collapse and the First World War finally ended, governments around the world found themselves having to deal with Marxism, not as a fringe movement that could be dismissed from serious consideration, but as a rising power that controlled the world's largest nation and was aggressively trying to spread itself over the rest of the world.

Almost three millennia of apocalyptic rhetoric lay ready at hand for the propaganda war that followed, and both sides pounced on it at once. Liberals across the industrial world in the years between the two World Wars inevitably hailed the Soviet Union in language originally crafted for the New Jerusalem; their conservative opponents found an equally useful stock of cant in traditional descriptions of the kingdom of the Antichrist. Rhetoric replaced reality as the Left found reasons to justify or ignore the gulags and mass murders of the Soviet regime, while the Right found as many reasons to justify or ignore the equivalent atrocities committed in the name of anti-communism. Outside the Second World War, when the Soviet Union and the nations of the West found themselves briefly and uncomfortably on the same side in a struggle against the one political system that was unquestionably worse than either, the great struggle between Marxism and its adversaries dominated world history throughout most of the twentieth century.

The rise and fall of Communism as a world power—it

would be as accurate to call it a world religion—has been analyzed in any number of books. Perhaps the most crucial point to take away from the long struggle, though, is that Marx's prophecies turned out to be quite simply wrong, in the simplest and most straightforward sense. At the peak of the Communist movement, something close to half the human beings on Earth lived in countries governed according to Marxist doctrines, but nowhere did the Utopian results Marx promised turn out to be forthcoming. In every Communist nation, instead, the dictatorship of the working class rapidly turned into a dictatorship like any other, and the state, far from withering away, turned into a sprawling, metastatic bureaucracy that enforced increasingly dysfunctional policies on an increasingly unhappy populace by means of a huge and efficient apparatus of secret police, labor camps, and mass murder.

Nor, of course, did history follow the straight line Marx and his followers sketched out for it. Instead, Communism reached its high-water mark in the 1960s and began to ebb rapidly thereafter. By the last decade of the twentieth century, the Soviet Union had imploded, the leadership of allegedly Communist China calmly embraced capitalism, and very nearly the only place Marxism retained any cachet at all was on the campuses of the more liberal universities in the United States.

This in itself is remarkable, because the United States was the one major industrial nation where Marxism found only very limited support during its heyday. Marxist political parties, major players in most other nations, found themselves relegated to the outermost fringes of American politics and culture. There was, at one point, a great deal of discussion about this "American exceptionalism," and historians and sociologists vied to promote their own explanations for Marxism's failure to thrive on American soil.

One important factor, though, did not always get as much attention as it deserved. People in America had very little interest in importing a secular Marxist version of the apocalyptic myth from overseas, because they had an abundance of apocalyptic options at home—and nearly all of these derived straight from the original religious context of the apocalypse meme.

CHAPTER FIVE:

EYES TURNED TOWARD HEAVEN

To this day, nobody is quite sure why religious habits of thought that lost most of their impact in Europe by the end of the eighteenth century stayed alive and potent in the United States. Still, that is unquestionably what happened, and fashions in apocalypse followed suit. Long after most Europeans had turned in search of salvation to radical nationalism or Marxism, a very large fraction of Americans still clung to the medieval faith that Christ would return in clouds of glory to inaugurate the millennium in the very near future.

The national faith in an imminent Second Coming sank roots into American soil early on. In the years right after

1720, when Puritan preacher Jonathan Edwards kick-started the Great Awakening with his blockbuster sermon "Sinners in the Hands of an Angry God," most of New England shuddered in the sort of delicious terror people nowadays get from watching zombie movies, half-convinced that the Earth was going to open up right underneath them as they sat in church and drop them straight into the gaping jaws of Hell. Like all subsequent revivals, the Great Awakening ran out of steam after a few years, as the people who had flocked in droves into the churches, hoping to hear themselves consigned ever more colorfully to eternal damnation for their sins, headed off to other entertainments instead. Within a generation, however, new revivals sprang up elsewhere, and nearly all of them embraced the same tried-and-true themes of Christian apocalyptic.

The traveling revival preacher with his tent full of excitable listeners and his hellfire-and-brimstone sermons thus took up an enduring place in American popular culture. Certain parts of the country became famous, or perhaps notorious, for the repeated bursts of evangelical fervor and apocalyptic fear that swept over them. One tract of upstate New York, along the route of the Erie Canal from Utica to Buffalo, saw so many revivals go through that it acquired the nickname of "the Burned-Over District."

These outbursts of religious enthusiasm drew heavily on a schism in American society that goes all the way back to colonial times, the enduring cultural divide between the cities along the coast and the farm country further inland. The wealth, relative political and social liberalism, and cosmopolitan attitudes of the urban culture of the coasts has always sparked resentment from the poorer, more conservative, and more patriotic hinterlands, and that resentment has been returned with interest. Revivals played to that schism with gusto, condemning the urban centers as so many Babylons that God would shortly smite, after which the supposedly more virtuous folk of the rural farm country would receive some suitably spiritualized version of all the enjoyments their urban rivals monopolized for the present.

Popular as it was, the revival phenomenon remained localized so long as America itself was a collection of local and regional cultures, each shaped primarily by its own distinctive colonial heritage. In the decades that followed the Revolutionary War, as the former colonies gradually merged into a nation and new technologies of transport and communications made it easier for people and ideas to move from one region to another, the potential scope of apocalyptic movements grew accordingly. Sooner or later, some such movement was bound to catch fire over a large fraction of the new republic and leap across the gap between the inland farming districts and the coastal intelligentsia. The one that finally did so was the Millerite movement.

$$\Omega$$

Behind this movement was one of America's first great waves of social reform. Beginning right after the War of 1812, many Americans embraced a flurry of liberal and radical causes: the abolition of slavery, women's rights, pacifism, temperance movements, and diet and dress reform, among many others. Boston was to the radicalism of that age what San Francisco would be to the comparable movement a century and a half later, and from Boston and the towns around it, earnest missionaries sallied forth to reform the world.

These were missionaries in every sense of the word, for American Christianity was anything but conservative in those days. Most of the leading reform organizations—the Anti-Slavery Societies, the Non-Resistant League (the great pacifist organization of the day), the Temperance League, and more—were allied with churches and staffed and supported by clergymen. It is no exaggeration to say that evangelical Protestantism was to the counterculture of the 1820s and 1830s what Eastern religions were to the counterculture of the 1960s.

It was into this setting that William Miller came with news of the imminent end of the world. Born in 1782, Miller was a farmer and Baptist lay preacher who turned to the Bible after a youthful flirtation with Deism. After years of intensive study of scripture, he became convinced that a verse in the Old Testament—Daniel 8:14, "And he said unto me, Unto two thousand and three hundred days; then shall the sanctuary be cleansed"—revealed the secret of time's imminent end. Twenty-three hundred days, according to the established Biblical interpretations of the time, meant twenty-three hundred years; counting from the restoration of the Jews to the Holy Land at the end of the Babylonian Captivity in 457 BCE, that gave 1843 as the time when "the sanctuary [would] be cleansed"—a metaphor Miller took to indicate nothing less than the Second Coming.

This date formed only one part of a complex theory of prophecy that mapped the events of the Books of Daniel and Revelation onto more than two thousand years of history. For Miller, as for many of his contemporaries, every major event in the history of the Christian world between the last page of the Book of Acts and the end of the world had been foretold in prophecy, and a great deal of effort had already gone into figuring out just what historical kingdom or event was represented by each scriptural symbol. Each of the ten toes of Daniel's colossal figure of gold, silver, brass, and iron, for example, had to be related to one of the kingdoms that emerged out of the Roman Empire when "the stone...cut out without hands" (Daniel 2:34) broke the image into pieces, and each of the seven trumpets of the Book of Revelation had to correspond to some historical happening.

Miller's system of prophecy adopted all these standard tools of interpretation. The only thing that set it apart from the calculations of other prophecy analysts in his time was his conviction that the end was close enough to be marked on the calendar. It was precisely Miller's acceptance of the standard religious tenets of his time that made his prediction so compelling to his contemporaries. As one historian of American apocalypticism, Whitney R. Cross, pointed out years ago, "the whole of American Protestantism came so very close to the same beliefs. Their [the Millerites'] doctrine was the logical absolute of fundamentalist orthodoxy."

Patient as only a New England farmer can be, Miller did not go public with his discovery right away. He spent years rechecking his figures and consulting historical and scriptural authorities, and only after more than a decade of careful calculation did he set out to publicize the news that the world would come to an end "sometime near 1843." For several years thereafter, he traveled the back roads of New England from one small church to another, spreading the word of the imminent end of time. In 1838, however, he met the Rev. Joshua V. Himes, and shortly thereafter found himself at the head of a mass movement.

Himes was one of the leading lights of the 1830s' Boston counterculture, a lively preacher active in very nearly every imaginable reform movement, and a consummate organizer and media manager. With Miller's blessing, he quickly took charge of publicizing and financing the message of the imminent Second Coming. In 1840, Himes launched the first Millerite newspaper, *Signs of the Times,* and soon followed it with a pamphlet series, *The Second Advent*, and an edition of Miller's lectures. In October of the same year, the first conference of the new movement brought hundreds of Millerites to Boston. Money poured in, the number of committed Millerites grew, and controversy over Miller's predictions filled newspapers and churches across the young nation.

One of the reasons why Millerism took off the way it did was precisely that it came on the heels of a movement for social reform just when that movement was faltering, and offered renewed hope to console the repeated failures of believers in change. By the end of the 1830s, it had become clear to most people that the Boston counterculture had accomplished nearly all of what it was going to accomplish; many of its proposed reforms had gone nowhere. Worse, two of the central causes of the time—the struggles against slavery and war—were on a collision course with each other, as it became agonizingly clear that an end to slavery in America would likely be obtained only at the cost of civil war. Those reformers who still longed for a perfect world, and there were still many of them at the beginning of the 1840s, were thus easy pickings for an ideology that told them they would get that world handed to them miraculously by God Himself in the very near future.

Millerism cashed in on their vulnerability with one of the first really massive media campaigns in American history. By 1843, when the movement was in full swing, Millerite papers included Boston's *Signs of the Times*, New York's *The Midnight Cry*, Philadelphia's *The Philadelphia Alarm*, and *The Western Midnight Cry* out of Cincinnati. Between newspaper issues, the Millerite presses turned out tracts, pamphlets, and posters outlining Miller's prophetic system in garish imagery. Between three and four hundred ministers were busy preaching the imminence of the Second Coming, and Himes himself was touring with the largest tent in America, a monster pavilion that could hold an audience of four thousand for sermons and lectures on Miller's predictions.

All this activity orbited around the dazzling conviction that Christ would come in glory, right in front of everyone on Earth, sometime between March 21, 1843, and March

21, 1844. Millerite leaders, very much including Miller himself, tried to avoid pinning the movement down to any one date; still, the demand for an exact date among ordinary Millerites was intense, and, in prophecy as in economics, supply rarely falls short of demand. As the last year of time began, Millerite preachers launched into what they believed would be their final round of tent revivals, lectures, and media blitzes before the world ended. All in all, some five million copies of Millerite publications saw print during the movement, which was a stunning total for the time, and a major factor in its popular success.

March 1844 came and went, however, with no sign of the promised Second Coming. Critics and scoffers had a field day. Miller, Himes, and their colleagues pointed out that the calculations allowed Christ a certain amount of wiggle room, and urged Millerite believers to stand fast in the certainty that they could expect the world to end sometime very soon. Himes added two new periodicals to the Millerite stable, the dense theological quarterly *Advent Shield and Review* and a women's magazine, the *Advent Message to the Daughters of Zion*. For the first time, he also began to advocate that Millerites who found themselves being ridiculed in their churches ought to leave and found new churches that would focus on the Millerite doctrine; the normal process by which sects are born was under way.

It was at this point, however, that the movement suddenly spun out of its leaders' control. The immediate cause was an obscure Millerite preacher, Rev. Samuel S. Snow, who became convinced that he had found a small error in one of the historical authorities Miller had used. Once corrected, according to Snow, Miller's calculations pointed inexorably to an exact date, October 22, 1844, the Day of Atonement in the Jewish calendar. Snow's announcement caused an explosion of excitement among Millerites. Miller and Himes tried to downplay the new date, but found that the movement they thought they were leading was quite prepared to find other leaders if the existing ones failed to provide it with what it wanted. As the summer of 1844 moved toward autumn, Snow's prediction found tens of thousands of eager listeners at Millerite camp meetings and revivals.

Miller apparently never quite accepted the new chronology, but Himes became convinced that the rising tide of excitement could only be the work of the Holy Spirit. On October 6, in front of a packed house at the Boston Tabernacle, he announced his conversion to the new date. A week later *The Advent Herald* published an announcement signed by Himes that this would be the paper's last edition, since the Second Coming of Christ would preempt any further issues.

During the last week or so before October 22, many thousands of Millerites across the country gave up all but the most necessary work, and devoted themselves night and day to prayer and Bible study to prepare to meet their heavenly judge. Some of them—the point has been the subject of fierce dispute—apparently made themselves white robes to wear, so that they would be appropriately dressed when they ascended bodily into heaven. The great majority of them—this point is less controversial rose before dawn on

October 22 and prayerfully climbed onto hilltops, in the hope of having the best possible view of Christ when he appeared in glory in the clouds.

When the Sun rose as usual on an unredeemed world on October 23, in turn, the Millerite movement imploded. Most of its members went back to their old churches, or went on to other new religious movements. A minority remained faithful to the Advent message, and gradually coalesced into an organized sect, which survives today after several additional mutations as the Seventh-Day Adventists. Miller himself remained convinced of the imminence of the Second Coming until his death in 1849. Himes remained active in Adventist circles until 1876, when he became an Episcopalian; he was ordained in 1878 and spent the remainder of his life serving in obscurity as a missionary in South Dakota.

"The Great Disappointment," as the Millerite fiasco came to be called, delivered a body blow to American apocalypticism that continued to be felt throughout the nineteenth century. While conservative Christians still spoke of Christ's imminent return, very few people wanted to be reminded of the consequences of taking that belief seriously enough to set a date for it. In response, as the century went on, a great many Christians adopted the reforming zeal of the 1830s and 1840s without its apocalyptic dimensions. The Social Gospel movement, which called on Christians to make the world a better place instead of waiting for the Second Coming to do it for them, became widespread.

Now and then, though, the Millerite message still found

its way to listening ears. In 1869 a young man named Charles Taze Russell attended a lecture by the Millerite minister Jonas Wendell, who had reset the date of the Second Coming for 1873. Inspired by the lecture, Russell started a Bible study group in Pittsburgh, Pennsylvania, and began his own systematic study of Bible prophecy. In the mid-1870s he became convinced that the solution to the prophetic riddle was the Second Coming had already happened—that Christ had returned, but invisibly—and, in 1877, together with Nelson Barbour, a Millerite preacher who had come to the same conclusion, he published a book entitled *The Three Worlds and the Harvest of This World*, proclaiming his interpretation of prophecy to a mostly uninterested world. Russell and Barbour parted company over theological differences in 1897, and at once Russell began to publish a magazine, *Zion's Watch Tower*, and to organize local congregations under the label "Bible Students."

In his voluminous writings, Russell stated that the period of Christ's invisible presence in the world would come to an end with an apocalyptic bang in 1914. Many of his followers saw the beginning of the First World War as proof of Russell's teachings, but when Russell himself died in 1916, no further divine manifestation followed. It was left to Russell's successor, Joseph Rutherford, who ended up in control of the movement after a flurry of political infighting in 1917 and 1918, to come up with an explanation for the 1914 failure. Russell's theories provided him with a good model, and before long the Watchtower Tract Society was claiming that the end of the world in 1914 was invisible, just as Christ's Second Coming in 1872 had been.

"Millions Now Living Will Never Die!" That was Rutherford's most famous slogan, one that was repeated constantly in Watchtower publications in the years between the two World Wars. In 1931, looking for a more distinctive name for his organization, he borrowed a turn of phrase from Isaiah 43:10 and renamed it the Jehovah's Witnesses. Years passed, the world failed to end, and the Jehovah's Witnesses are still preaching the imminent arrival of the end of the world, but at this point they have settled down to become another small denomination in the patchwork fabric of American religion.

$$\Omega$$

Well before the Great Disappointment came and went, however, the ideas that would drive the next great wave of Protestant Christian apocalypticism were already taking shape. Their creator was John Nelson Darby (1800–1882), an Irish Protestant minister who left the Church of Ireland shortly after his ordination in 1825, and eventually ended up as the head of his own sect, the Plymouth Brethren. Darby was a tireless lecturer with a bundle of original ideas, and his reinterpretation of the apocalypse meme caught on rapidly.

His central innovation was an ingenious response to the trap that caught William Miller, the insistence that the entire history of the world from the Crucifixion to the Second Coming had to be predicted by the Bible. Darby's system of Dispensationalism divides history into different periods, or dispensations, which each represent a particular way that God deals with humanity. The Bible, Darby held, has plenty to say about the dispensations that occurred up to and including the crucifixion of Jesus, and nearly as much to say about the ones that will follow once the events of the Book of Revelation begin.

What it does not discuss in anything like the same detail is another dispensation—the Church Age, or Great Paren-thesis—which falls between these two points. The Church Age, according to Darby, began when the Holy Spirit descended on the apostles at Pentecost, and will continue until the opening events of the Book of Revelation, when the stopwatch of prophecy starts to tick once again and the apocalypse is on.

Instead of trying to shoehorn the world's history into the ornate framework of the Book of Revelation, in other words, Dispensationalism allowed all the events of John's vision to be set in the future and treated in the most literal terms, and it dodged the bullet of date-setting while still allowing Dispensationalist preachers to claim that the end was breathing down humanity's neck. The fact that it took the most tortured kinds of logic to extract the doctrine of the Great Parenthesis from the Bible was the only difficulty with this ingenious scheme, and that difficulty seems to have given Darby and his many successors no second thoughts.

A second major innovation turned out to be equally central to the success of Darby's new apocalyptic theology: the Rapture. Based on one ambiguous verse in the New Testament—I Thessalonians 4:17, "Then we which are alive and remain shall be caught up together with them in the clouds, to meet the Lord in the air; and so shall we ever be with the Lord"—the doctrine of the Rapture is the belief that at the moment when the Church Age ends and the events of the Book of Revelation start to happen, all true Christians will suddenly vanish, body and soul, to meet Christ in the air, while everyone else on Earth will be left to suffer the horrors John of Patmos predicted for the world in its last days. It was a brilliant innovation; the notion of having an instant ticket off the planet to heaven, while everyone else gets to suffer seven years of torment, proved just as popular as the Millerite dream of the skies suddenly opening to reveal Jesus to the world.

By the middle years of the nineteenth century, accordingly, the Great Parenthesis had begun to fill the gap left open by the Great Disappointment, and provided evangelical preachers all over the English-speaking world with plenty of ammunition for the old sport of scaring the bejesus out of their congregations. The predominance of the Social Gospel among mainstream denominations and keen memories of the Millerite debacle meant that for many years, Darby's disciples labored on the fringes of the Christian world, finding most of their converts among the poor and disenfranchised. In the soaring optimism of the period Mark Twain christened "the Gilded Age," when technological progress, imperial expansion, and Utopian political schemes filled many people's minds in America and Europe alike with dreams of glory anchored firmly in this world, preachers of an imminent Second Coming found few listeners.

That began to change in the first years of the twentieth century, as power struggles between European empires launched the rising spiral of crises that finally exploded in the summer of 1914 in the opening volleys of the First World War. By that time the Millerite fiasco had faded from America's collective memory, and Dispensationalist preachers found that the temper of the times was shifting in their favor. Innovative marketing campaigns that borrowed heavily from the media advertising methods of the time enabled the apocalyptic message to spread far and wide. When a group of devoutly Dispensationalist oil barons funded a series of pamphlets titled *The Fundamentals*, which were distributed by the millions of copies across America, the movement found a name and a party line.

By the early 1920s, fundamentalism was a rising force in American religion and culture, and formed pragmatic alliances with other groups on the conservative end of society. The Ku Klux Klan was among the most important of these allies. The original Klan had been a Southern guerrilla movement opposing Reconstruction, which was crushed by federal troops and courts during President Grant's administration. It was revived in 1915 as a vehicle for racist, anti-Catholic, and anti-immigrant activism, and quickly gained more than a Southern following, with a very strong presence in the Midwest and the West Coast. In the early 1920s, when the revived Klan was at its height, some forty thousand fundamentalist ministers were proud card-carrying Klansmen, and twenty-six of the thirty-nine Klokards (state lecturers paid by the Klan to promote its ideas) were ministers of fundamentalist churches. The Rev. E. F. Stanton, a fundamentalist minister, thus saw nothing inappropriate in writing a book entitled *Christ and Other Klansmen, or, Lives of Love*, which was published in 1924 to rave reviews in the right-wing media.

Alliance with the Ku Klux Klan, however, turned into a huge liability for fundamentalist churches when the Klan all but collapsed in a series of juicy scandals in the late 1920s. The involvement of such leading fundamentalist figures as Rev. Aimee Semple McPherson in colorful scandals of their own did not help matters. The Great Depression put another round of nails in the coffin of the fundamentalist movement, as conservative economic policies that were backed by fundamentalist ministers and media failed to do anything to the economic troubles of that time other than make them worse. By the mid-1930s, fundamentalism was in headlong retreat. It took forty years and the cultural revolutions of the 1960s to breathe new life into the surviving fundamentalist churches and give them a platform for their apocalyptic dreams.

Ω

One consequence of the rise of Dispensationalism was a renewal of the old sport of hunting the Antichrist. This had never quite fallen by the wayside, even during the heyday of secular optimism; one wag during the American Revolution calculated that the phrase "Royal Supremacy in Britain" in Hebrew worked out to 666, while Tolstoy's

War and Peace includes a scene in which Pierre adds up the phrase "l'Empereur Napoleon" and gets the same inevitable sum. Still, all these ingenious speculations had to contend with the conviction, all but universal among nineteenth-century Protestants, that the Antichrist was none other than the Pope.

This notion was adopted without question by Darby's original followers, and remained standard among Dispensationalists even when the unification of Italy stripped the Vatican of the last of its once-mighty political and military power and left the Pope the undisputed ruler of a few small neighborhoods in Rome. This did not faze the more traditionally minded evangelicals; shortly after John F. Kennedy's election in 1960, Dispensationalist preacher J. Dwight Pentecost drew on the old Pope-Antichrist equation in denouncing the new president's Catholicism, while Hal Lindsey in *The Late Great Planet Earth* predicted the Papacy's return to secular power as a proponent of the international peace and prosperity schemes that formed the Antichrist's expected platform.

Still, as the twentieth century drew on, new candidates for the post were clearly needed, and the law of supply and demand active elsewhere in the history of prophecy quickly furnished them. Adolf Hitler got some attention as a potential Antichrist, especially when some thoughtful soul figured out that if you assign each English letter a three-digit number, with A=100, B=101, C=102, and so on through the alphabet, the name "Hitler" adds to 666. During the heyday of Communism, Lenin and Stalin also got a certain amount of attention as possible candidates, though most Dispensationalist writers preferred to assign Russia its traditional role as Gog, the kingdom of the north, and looked for the Antichrist elsewhere.

The most popular candidate for the Antichrist in the years between the two World Wars, in fact, was Benito Mussolini. The Italian dictator's insistence that he was restoring the Roman Empire and his avid pursuit of the media spotlight, were read by many Dispensationalist writers as likely signs that Mussolini was in fact the long-awaited Beast. One evangelical writer with a taste for conspiracy theory pointed out that the fasces, the ancient Roman emblem Mussolini had adopted for his Fascist party, had been put on US dimes starting in the early years of the twentieth century, and suggested on this basis that plans for the Antichrist's world dominion were already well underway.

The sorry showing of Mussolini's would-be empire in the Second World War removed him from consideration, but plenty of other options presented themselves thereafter. Cold War maneuvering between the American and Soviet blocs, followed by the energy crises of the seventies and the emergence of OPEC, made the Middle East a fertile source of candidates. Two successive presidents of Egypt, Gamal Abdel Nasser and Anwar el-Sadat, were discussed feverishly in the Dispensationalist literature as possible Antichrists, and of course Saddam Hussein, during the years when he was America's favorite whipping boy in the Middle East, was the hands-down favorite for the Antichrist as well.

Other writers in the prophecy business looked further

afield. Henry Kissinger, whose name in Hebrew adds to 111, was widely discussed as a potential Antichrist in the Seventies. The birthmark on the forehead of Mikhail Gorbachev sparked more than occasional references to the Mark of the Beast, though these faded away after the Soviet Union collapsed under Gorbachev's management. For an Antichrist, this was not exactly promising, though it's curious to note that the vast majority of political figures selected as potential Antichrists by American prophecy writers in the twentieth century ended their careers with embarrassing flops of one kind or another.

Still, these failures were more than counterbalanced in the years following the Second World War by two events that seemed to suggest that the old prophecy had sprouted new teeth. The first was the flash of light over Hiroshima that announced the dawn of the atomic age. A great many people not otherwise attracted to the apocalypse meme found few if any alternatives to help them make sense of weapons that were almost literally apocalyptic in their effects. Prophecy writers in America and elsewhere were quick to jump on the nuclear bandwagon, revising their predictions of global war and the coming of the Antichrist to include mushroom clouds and atomic blackmail. All through the Cold War, it became very nearly an article of faith among evangelical Christians that the End Times would involve a nuclear war between the United States and the Soviet Union.

The second event that gave the apocalypse meme its post-Second World War boost was the founding of the modern state of Israel in 1947. To a great many writers on prophecy, the return of the Jews to the Holy Land had long been one of the crucial signs of the imminence of Armageddon, and the establishment of a Jewish state in Palestine seemed to them to be both a stunning confirmation of the old prediction and a red-alert signal that the End Times were near. It's rarely recalled that Dispensationalist churches all through the first half of the twentieth century played a huge role in setting the stage for Israel's founding, by advocating for Jewish settlement in Palestine, and pressing the British and American governments to support the project. Equally, the migration of Jewish survivors from post-Nazi Europe to Palestine was simply the latest and largest of a long line of such movements in the wake of persecution; it's worth noting as well that the role that Dispensationalists assigned to the Jews of Israel—that of being slaughtered en masse by the Antichrist, on the one hand, or converting to Christianity upon Jesus's reappearance on the other—is not exactly what the founders of Israel had in mind for their people. Still, such considerations did nothing to dispel the popularity of the Dispensationalist vision of the imminent End Times among America's Protestant Christians.

Ω

As the twentieth century drew toward its end, these trends and many others helped spark a second wave of American fundamentalism all but identical to the one that crested and broke in the 1920s. The profound social changes of the 1960s shocked many formerly liberal Americans to the core, and made many of them ready to listen to preachers who identified these shifts as signs that this time, the end was really, truly, finally at hand. The same mass marketing techniques that helped drive the first wave of fundamentalism, retooled for new technologies, found work promoting a new generation of televangelists and fundamentalist political causes.

With the election of Ronald Reagan as president in 1980, fundamentalist leaders found themselves welcome in Washington DC, not least because their grassroots church-to-church networking had proven itself to be a powerful tool to get out the vote for Republican candidates. This newfound political clout, though, did nothing to soften the fundamentalists' conviction of living in the End Times, in a world that was predestined to run amuck once the Antichrist showed up and took control.

It's important to remember that even among conservative American Protestants, not everyone climbed aboard the Dispensationalist bandwagon. One notable exception was David Wilkerson, author of *The Cross and the Switchblade*—a bestselling account of his work with teen gang members in New York City—and popular evangelical preacher. Wilkerson argued forcefully that fixating on the apocalypse meme was getting in the way of a more important struggle: "The war we need to focus on right now is the one taking place in our own hearts…our battle isn't with the beast of John's revelation, but with the beast within us!"

Still, such arguments fell mostly on deaf ears. It's symptomatic of the impact of Dispensationalism that one of the bestselling authors of the 1970s was Hal Lindsey, a Protestant minister who resigned from a position with Campus Crusade for Christ to write the first of several wildly popular books on the end of the world. *The Late Great Planet Earth*, which first saw print in 1970, retailed the standard Dispensationalist take on the Book of Revelation so exactly that others who attended Dallas Theological Seminary with Lindsey in the late 1960s complained publicly that his book was little more than a rehash of the lectures they and Lindsey had taken in at that institution.

Central to Lindsey's strategy was the familiar claim that current political events proved that the Rapture, the Tribulation, and the Millennium were about to arrive. As political conditions changed, Lindsey produced book after book, each announcing in the same shrill tones that current events—whatever they happened to be—proved that the Second Coming could be expected any day now. In the usual way, in turn, each round of predictions was quietly forgotten once it turned out to be inaccurate: *The 1980s: Countdown to Armageddon*, with its insistence that the Rapture would occur in that decade, was quietly replaced in the early 1990s with *Planet Earth—2000 AD*, which insisted with equal force that Christians could expect to be raptured off the planet before the turn of the millennium.

Lindsey was far from the only evangelical Protestant author to build a lucrative career by preaching the imminent end of time. Christian humorist Barbara Johnson, for example, released a very successful book about the Rapture with an unfortunate title—*He's Gonna Toot And I'm Gonna*

Scoot—that made most unbelievers think of flatulence rather than apocalyptic theology. Far and away the greatest success story of them all, though, was the sprawling series of Christian apocalyptic thriller novels, authored by longtime end-of-the-world preacher Tim LaHaye and novelist Jerry Jenkins, which began with 1995's *Left Behind* and continued through fifteen other volumes, selling in excess of sixty-five million copies to date.

The premise of the *Left Behind* series was as clever as it was simple. After the Rapture, LaHaye and Jenkins reasoned, some few people who had previously doubted the truth of Christianity might reconsider their beliefs and turn to Jesus in the face of the miraculous disappearance of all true Christians and the onset of the Tribulation. Several of these Christians by virtue of second thoughts provided the series with its main characters, and the events of the seven years from the Rapture to the Second Coming, drawn straight out of Dispensationalist theology, supplied the plot and most of the scenery. Unlike most previous novels set in the End Times—there had been many, dating back to 1903—LaHaye and Jenkins had the good sense to keep their story lines fast-paced and suspenseful, modeling their novels on the popular thriller novels of the time, so that the theology—which is admittedly ladled out with a very large spoon—is less indigestible than in most equivalent books.

The huge popularity of the *Left Behind* series cemented the Rapture and the rest of Dispensationalist theory in place as the standard version of the apocalypse meme for most American Christians. Its appeal was by no means universal, theologians from outside the Dispensationalist fold sniped at it from various angles, while one disgruntled evangelical Christian showed the same dubious talent for titles as Barbara Johnson, and launched a website entitled *Exposing Satan's Left Behind*, leaving unbelievers to wonder why a Christian would want to uncover any part of Lucifer's posterior.

Still, as of this writing a very large fraction of American Christians remain convinced that sometime very soon they will abruptly disappear from the face of the planet, leaving the rest of us to fill supporting roles in a thriller with the Antichrist as the special guest star. Bumper stickers saying "Warning: In case of Rapture, this car will be unoccupied" remain a common sight on America's highways, while a handful of ingenious promoters are currently offering Rapture pet care services, offering—in exchange for cash up front—to take in the pets of believers when they are whisked away to meet Jesus in the clouds.

Ω

Well before the Rapture became a staple of popular culture among America's evangelical Protestants and a staple of popular humor elsewhere in American society, though, versions of the apocalypse meme that drew on Christian traditions had already started to encounter competition from other versions of the same meme with roots that lay much further afield. A good many of these emerged in the far reaches of American spirituality, though few of them stayed there. There had been plenty of alternative spiritual traditions on the fringes of American society, all the way back to the alchemists and hexenmeisters of colonial days, but they played a very minor role in American apocalyptic until the second half of the twentieth century, when some of the same factors that drove the rebirth of Christian fundamentalism sparked apocalyptic movements that, in some cases, found a popularity the traditions that launched them never managed on their own.

Far and away the most influential of these upwardly mobile apocalyptic movements was the one that emerged, beginning in 1947, in response to widespread sightings of unidentified objects in the skies above America and, later on, much of the rest of the world. More than six decades after the original 1947 "flying saucer" scare, the UFO debate remains as divisive as ever, and the two viewpoints that have come to dominate that debate—the belief that UFOs are alien spacecraft from some distant planet, on the one hand, and the belief that everyone who claims to have seen a UFO is mistaken, delusional, or lying, on the other— are far from the only, or even the most likely, of the possible explanations.

Though the origins and nature of the UFO phenomenon remain controversial, its role as raw material for the apocalypse meme is not. In the earliest days of the subculture that sprang up around UFO sightings, the idea that the flying saucers had appeared to warn Earthlings about the risk of self-destruction via nuclear war was a central topic of discussion. By the early 1950s, the seeds of the apocalypse meme hidden in that idea had sprouted into luxuriant growth, and people who believed that they were in tele-pathic contact with alien astronauts—and there were quite a few people who made such claims at the time—vied with one another in issuing colorful proclamations of the imminent doom from which the Space Brothers were about to save us.

One such prophetess unwittingly helped create a modern classic in the literature of sociology. Her name was Dorothy Martin, a suburban Chicago housewife turned UFO contactee, and in 1954 she announced that aliens from the planet Clarion had told her that North America would be ravaged by catastrophic floods on December 21 of that year. Newspaper coverage of the prediction caught the attention of a team of sociologists at the University of Minnesota, and they arranged for several graduate students to go undercover and join Martin's small group of followers, to see what would happen.

What happened, to summarize a very long story, was the story of the Millerites, reduced to the scale of a suburban backyard. Just as William Miller's followers stood on hilltops waiting for Christ to appear in glory in the clouds, Martin's dozen or so followers gathered on the evening of December 20th, feverishly removed every scrap of metal from their clothing in accordance with the instructions Martin believed the aliens had sent her, and waited vainly through the night for a flying saucer to swoop down and carry them off into the skies. Like the Millerites, in turn, Martin's group disintegrated after the failure of its prophecy; Martin went on to a long career as a minor New Age teacher, and most of the other members returned to their ordinary lives. The researchers' account of these events, published in 1956 under the title *When Prophecy Fails,* gave Martin the pseudonym of Marion Keech and concealed the identities of the group's other members by similar means; it remains to this day one of the best accounts of the trajectory of an apocalyptic group from the announcement of prophecy to the humiliation that follows its failure.

Not all of the apocalyptic UFO groups that followed in the footsteps of Dorothy Martin ended so harmlessly. On the morning of March 26, 1997, police officers alerted by neighbors searched a San Diego mansion and found the corpses of thirty-nine men and women, all dead of self-administered poison. One of them was Marshall Applewhite, who had been active in the UFO-contactee scene since 1972, and the rest were his followers, who formed a sect that called itself "Heaven's Gate." After a long series of unfulfilled predictions that the Space Brothers would descend and lift them all to the "Evolutionary Level Above Human," Applewhite proclaimed in late 1996 that Comet Hale-Bopp would soon crash into the Earth and annihilate the human race, and he and his followers apparently decided to make sure that in their case, at least, the prophecy would come true. It's unlikely, to use no stronger word, that their decision to "shed their physical containers" got them seats onboard the giant spaceship they believed was hovering in Hale-Bopp's tail, but it did spare them the embarrassment of having to explain away yet another failed prediction of the end.

Ω

Few of the apocalyptic movements of late twentieth-century America ended as wretchedly as Heaven's Gate, but failed prophecies and disappointed prophets were common enough. The widespread belief that the Sixties marked the imminent onset of a new and much happier age of the world is as good an example as any. Much of the raw material for this notion, interestingly enough, came straight out of the original starlore that gave birth to the apocalypse meme itself so many centuries before.

Astrology, which had a lively following across Europe during the years when the first European settlements in the New World took root, found a home in America early on. Long before independence, plenty of Americans had learned to plant by the phases of the Moon and anticipate the events of their lives from the positions of the planets at their birth. The popularity of astrology had waxed and waned since then, but it had never quite managed to lose its place in American culture, and the tumult of the Sixties happened to burst on the scene at a time when interest in astrology was on the upswing.

Still, what the Sixties' counterculture made of the archaic lore of the stars was nothing that the star-watchers of ancient times would have recognized. The idea that a new astrological age of the world was dawning, or had dawned, or would be dawning sometime soon, had been in circulation in the Western world for more than a century when the cultural ferment of the Sixties kicked off, and a variety of forecasts—some optimistic, others less so—circulated among the astrological cognoscenti. As these spilled out into popular culture in the late 1960s, though, the new phase of time's great wheel suddenly found itself redefined, and the Age of Aquarius was turned into yet another label for the same glowing Utopian fantasy that had been retailed under so many other brand names before its time.

When the Sixties ground to a halt without turning the world into one big love-in, those who had acquired a taste for apocalypse quickly found new fodder. Secular versions of the Age of Aquarius had repeated flurries of popularity, most of which drew heavily on the Baby Boom generation's remarkable faith in its own overwhelming historical importance. In 1970, Charles Reich published *The Greening of America*; 1980 saw the publication of Marilyn Ferguson's *The Aquarian Conspiracy*; in 2000, it was the turn of Paul H. Ray and Sherry Ruth Anderson, whose book was *Cultural Creatives*; each of these bestselling books proclaimed, in essence, that the then-current activities of the Boomers—redefined by these authors, respectively, as Consciousness III, the Aquarian Conspiracy, and the Cultural Creatives—marked the arrival of a great turning point in human history which would transform the world any day now. Hardcore secular apocalyptic also had its day in the sun, fostered in the Eighties by the antinuclear movement, and in the late 1990s by a much more heterogeneous movement that sprang up in response to the so-called Y2K crisis, the theory that the world's computer systems would freeze up on the morning of January 1, 2000.

More broadly, the decades just before the new millennium were a good time to be in the apocalypse business, and some highly innovative arguments got pressed into the service of the meme. One of the most interesting results was the belief in the Singularity. Originally proposed by science fiction writer Vernor Vinge and most loudly proclaimed in the writings of archetypal computer geek Ray Kurzweil, the Singularity is supposedly the result of inevitable future advances in artificial intelligence. According to the theory, human beings will soon be able to create intelligent computers that are smarter than we are; those computers, being smarter than we are, will then be able to create new computers that are even smarter, and so on, in a feedback loop that results in unimaginably intelligent machines capable of doing more or less anything.

The creation of these latter machines marks the Singularity. At that point, because nobody today is smart enough to figure out what super-intelligent computer minds will do, our ability to predict the future is extremely limited—a detail that has not stopped Kurzweil, at least, from waxing rhapsodic about the marvelous things that will happen once we hand over the world to the computerized mega-minds of the future. After the Singularity, Kurzweil has claimed, we can confidently expect human minds to be uploaded into immortal robot bodies, which will then go zooming off to experience an eternity of bliss in the infinite realms of outer space.

These notions, and the entire concept of the Singularity, have been sharply and cogently criticized by a great many specialists in the relevant sciences. Still, it hasn't often been noted that Kurzweil's Singularity narrative isn't actually a scientific theory at all; rather, it's a remarkably precise duplicate of John Nelson Darby's theology of the Rapture, rewritten in the language of science fiction. The Singularity is simply a technological remake of the Second Coming, with super-intelligent computers playing the role of God; Kurzweil's robot bodies correspond to the glorified bodies of the Christian elect, outer space to heaven, and so on, point for point. Kurzweil has predicted that the Singularity will arrive in 2045; if his prophecy has attracted any significant number of believers by then, the possibility that crowds will gather around artificial-intelligence laboratories like so many Millerites, waiting for their immortal robot bodies, can't be dismissed out of hand.

Despite all the blandishments of scientific or pseudo-scientific mythology, however, apocalyptic predictions based on astrology and mysticism retained a large following in the last years of the twentieth century. Among the most popular sources of these prophecies was Michel de Nostredame, usually known by the Latin form of his name, Nostradamus. A French astrologer and physician of Jewish descent who lived in the sixteenth century, Nostradamus began publishing an annual almanac of prophecies in 1550, and soon supplemented it with his famous *Centuries*, sets of one hundred quatrains (four-line verses) prophesying the future. Highly obscure and mostly free from inconvenient dates, his quatrains have been a rich source for would-be prophets ever since, with no more success than usual; one popular English translation of the *Centuries* from the 1990s, for example, insisted on the basis of two unusually murky quatrains that Edward Kennedy would inevitably be elected president of the United States.

While this prediction can hardly be laid at Nostradamus's own door, the few dated predictions he made on his own account have fared no better. The preface to the first edition of the *Centuries*, for example, states in no uncertain terms that Europe would be so drastically depopulated by floods and other causes before 1732 that much of its farmland would remain untilled for centuries thereafter. More famous, perhaps, was the "Great King of Terror" who was supposed to put in an appearance in the skies as the century ended:

> In the year 1999 and seven months
> From the sky will come a great king of terror
> To resuscitate the great king of Angouleme;
> Before and after, Mars reigns at his will.

There was accordingly a modest flurry of apocalyptic prediction in the months leading up to July 1999, though it was nearly drowned out by the furor surrounding the Y2K problem. When the "Great King of Terror" failed to show up on schedule and Mars showed no particular interest in reigning, those who had interpreted the prophecy in terms of nuclear war or asteroid impact did the usual thing, and went looking for some new prediction of doom. Many of them found it in a set of prophecies supposedly passed down from the ancient Maya.

This version of the apocalypse myth first began to surface in the 1970s, but it broke into public view in the wake of the Harmonic Convergence in 1987. This was the brainchild of Tony Shearer, a Lakota author and mystic whose studies of ancient Mexican myth convinced him, as so many others had convinced themselves before him, that he had figured out the secret key to the future. According to Shearer's 1975 book *Beneath the Moon and Under the Sun*, the history of Mexico from ancient times to the present was governed by a sequence of thirteen heavens and nine hells, each of which corresponded to the tzolkin, the fifty-two-year calendar cycle of ancient Mesoamerica. According to Shearer, the nine cycles of hell began more or less with the arrival of the conquistador Hernan Cortes on the shores of Mexico on April 21, 1519, and would therefore come to an end on August 16, 1987.

As it happens, there aren't the right number of days between these two dates to make up exactly nine tzolkin cycles, but this didn't stop Shearer's prophecy from turning into a media event on an international scale. It had plenty of help in doing so, particularly from New Age writer José Argüellés, who coined the term "Harmonic Convergence" for the 1987 date and wove it into a complicated theory about the future derived from the ancient Mayan calendar. By the time the date of the Harmonic Convergence arrived, hundreds of thousands of people had gathered at sacred sites around the world, waiting for something to happen.

When they went back home afterward, nothing much had happened, but there was an explanation ready at hand, courtesy of Argüellés's freshly published book *The Mayan Factor: Path Beyond Technology*. In that book, Argüellés claimed that the Harmonic Convergence marked the beginning of a transition out of the nine hell cycles—a transition that would reach its culmination when the Mayan calendar came to an end on December 21, 2012. With that pronouncement, Argüellés set in motion what may well be the defining apocalyptic furor of the twenty-first century.

CHAPTER SIX:

THE CURRENT CONTENDERS

The densely printed pages of *The National Interest,* an austere periodical mostly read by foreign policy wonks, are hardly a place you would expect to run across apocalyptic prophecy. Still, subscribers who opened their copies of the Summer 1989, issue were treated to one of the weirder offshoots of the apocalypse meme in living memory. The proclamation in question was an essay titled "The End of History?", and its author was Francis Fukuyama, a minor official in the US State Department turned neo-Hegelian philosopher; its appearance in print makes as good a marker as any for the beginning of today's apocalyptic frenzy.

"Frenzy," to be fair, may not seem like a plausible description for Fukuyama's thick prose and heavily foot-noted argument. Borrowing Hegel's notion of history as a linear process that moves from the clash of contradictions to their resolution on a higher level, Fukuyama identified the motive force of history as the struggle between competing systems of political economy, leading eventually to the triumph of the best possible system. That triumph, he argued, had just occurred with the collapse of the Soviet Union and the downfall of Communism. Liberal democracy—by which Fukuyama meant, more or less, the middle-of-the-road Republican stance of the first Bush administration—was therefore the best possible system of political economy, and history was therefore over. In the decades to come, those nations that had not yet adopted something like the American model of government and economics would inevitably do so, and thereafter the world would bask in a long afternoon of peace and plenty.

That this pronouncement was taken seriously at the time—and it was taken seriously, at least to the extent of sparking a flurry of scholarly debate and spawning several anthologies full of articles pro and con—does not speak well for the historical common sense of our age. Now it's true that we have no way of knowing how many distinguished academics laughed themselves into hiccups in private over Fukuyama's implied portrayal of George H. W. Bush, of all people, as Hegel's "world-historical personality," but the thundering irony in Fukuyama's announcement should have been lost on nobody.

Not that many years before his essay saw print, after all, the claim that history was chugging ahead toward some glorious and permanent fulfillment was the distinctive stock in trade of the Communist movement that Fukuyama, in his paper, had consigned to history's dustbin. So, of course, was the sort of flattening out of history into a single, one-dimensional conflict that was a central theme of Fukuyama's argument, and so, above all, was Hegel. All these things had been critiqued fiercely, and not inappropriately, by such conservative intellectuals as Eric Voegelin and Karl Popper back in the days when Fukuyama was still playing with toy trucks. The publication of "An End to History?" thus marked the point at which, at least in America, the conservative movement—which drew so heavily on Edmund Burke's magisterial arguments in opposition to the apocalypse meme—finally capitulated to it.

Conservatives, to be fair, are far from the only group in contemporary America who have found themselves swept up in the overfamiliar vortex of hope and dread that marks an apocalyptic movement in full spate. Plenty of devout Christians are still waiting for the Antichrist to man up and make his long-delayed appearance, with or without the benefit of the Rapture. Computer geeks still look forward to the Singularity. Believers in the imminent mass arrival of Space Brothers from other planets, who will usher in a Utopian age, clash now and again with believers in the imminent mass arrival of sinister alien Grays who have been abducting and molesting human beings for decades, if not centuries, while preparing to take over Earth for their own

151

nefarious purposes. Still, far and away the most colorful of the prophecies of approaching doom and salvation that was being retailed as the scholarly furor over Fukuyama's paper died down was the one that predicted that the end of the thirteenth baktun of the ancient Mayan calendar would also mark the end of the world.

$$\Omega$$

To understand the origins of the 2012 phenomenon, it's important to grasp the extent to which current knowledge about the ancient Maya has expanded in recent decades. During the middle decades of the twentieth century, outside the Soviet Union and its satellites, Mayan studies were dominated by the colorful personality of the redoubtable Sir Eric Thompson, a brilliant but utterly mistaken scholar whose work brought progress in Mayan research to a dead halt for four decades. The world's premier expert on all matters Mayan, and in particular the Mayan hieroglyphs, Thompson was also an archetypal British conservative, rabidly anti-Communist in politics and High Church Anglican in religion. To him, the ancient Mayans inhabited a golden age; he believed that the Mayan city-states had been ruled by peaceful astronomer-priests, who spent their days in theological debate and their nights contemplating the heavens, and who used their hieroglyphs solely to record abstruse mystical teachings that probably would never be decoded.

Under the influence of these beliefs, Thompson proceeded to use his very considerable prestige in the field of Mayan studies and his mastery of debating tactics to squash the career of anyone who disagreed with this assessment. Until well after his death in 1975, as a result, nearly everything published for popular audiences in the English-speaking world about the ancient Mayans followed the Thompson party line.

The New Age movement in America took shape while Thompson's views still dominated the scene, but put its own distinctive spin on the subject. Thompson's Mayan astronomer-priests, who bore a suspicious resemblance to Anglican bishops and vicars, suddenly found themselves transformed into New Age mystics, "surfers of the Zuvuya" who had grasped the ultimate secrets of the cosmos— including the date of its end. It's par for the course that Sir Eric Thompson's ideas about the ancient Maya remain glued in place in New Age circles, even though nearly every detail he claimed to have proved has been disproven by the unshakable testimony of the ancient Maya themselves, and that his 1954 book *The Rise and Fall of Maya Civilization* regularly appears in bibliographies of books supporting the 2012 phenomenon, while more recent and far more accurate books such as Linda Schele and David Friedel's *A Forest of Kings* tend to be notable by their absence. The reason is simple: their books don't feed the apocalypse meme, while Thompson's does.

Thus December 21, 2012, 4 Ahau 3 Kankin 13.0.0.0.0, when the thirteenth baktun of the current cycle comes to an end and the first baktun of the next cycle begins, has become the most fashionable apocalypse date just at the moment, and spawned a contemporary movement at least as influential in our time as the Millerites were in theirs. The difficulty in all this is simply that Thompson's fantasies about the ancient Maya have not merely been challenged but completely overthrown. The feat he considered impossible—the complete translation and interpretation of the Mayan hieroglyphs—was already beginning to take place during his lifetime, and shifted into overdrive once his death got the main obstacle out of the way.

The core breakthrough was actually made back in the 1950s by Russian linguist Yuri V. Knorosov, who showed that Mayan hieroglyphics—like Egyptian hieroglyphics, Chinese characters, and most other early writing systems—were a sophisticated form of picture writing in which some images were used to represent sounds and others were used for ideas. (It's very much as though someone were to write the English sentence "I love you" by drawing a picture of an eye, a heart, and a ewe.) Scholars following up on Knorosov's breakthrough discovered that the Mayan hieroglyphs recorded historical and religious texts in an ancient form of Chorti, one of the modern Mayan languages. Over ninety-five percent of all Mayan texts are now as readable as they were the day when they were written, and Mayan history, prophecy, and religion are no longer subjects for speculation, as the ancient Mayans themselves can have the last word on them.

One of the things that became very clear as a result of the decipherment of the Mayan hieroglyphs is exactly how much attention the ancient Mayans paid to the end of the thirteenth baktun. It apparently didn't interest them at all. There is precisely one Mayan inscription, among all of the thousands that survive, which even mentions the date. This is on Stela 6 at Tortuguero, a minor Mayan ruin in the Mexican state of Tabasco, and it runs as follows:

> *The thirteenth baktun will be finished*
> *Four Ahau, three Kankin*
> [illegible] *will occur*
> [it will be] *the descent of Bolon Yok'te Ku to* [illegible].

That's all. Bolon Yok'te Ku is a Mayan god; his name means "Nine Foot Tree" and it's been suggested that he has some relationship to the world tree, an important symbol in traditional Mayan spirituality, but nobody knows for sure. He isn't the most important Mayan god by a long shot; his descent is far from the most colorful event predicted for the future in Mayan inscriptions; and—it bears repeating—this one passing reference on one stela at one minor Mayan site is the only reference anywhere in the whole body of Mayan inscriptions to December 21, 2012. This is all the more striking in that there are many hundreds of other inscriptions talking about dates in the future; a fair number of them—despite endlessly repeated claims in New Age literature—look forward to dates well after 2012; and the great majority of them include prophecies about what gods or goddesses will do on those dates, many of which are a good deal more colorful than the one for 2012.

There's a good example in one of the most famous of all

Mayan buildings, the Temple of Inscriptions at Palenque. Now that Mayan hieroglyphs can be read, we know that this building's name when it was built was Bolon-Et-Nah, the House of Nine Images, and it was the tomb of Hanab-Pacal II, Kul Ahau ("Holy Lord") of the kingdom we call Palenque and the Mayans called Bak, the Bone Kingdom.

Hanab-Pacal II is as firmly rooted in history as any Roman emperor or American president. Inscriptions in his tomb tell us that he was born on March 26, 603, ascended the throne of Palenque on July 29, 615, and fought a series of successful wars against the rival Mayan kingdoms of Calakmul and Bonampak. He then settled down to a busy middle age as a patron of the arts and architecture. His final project, started around 675, was his own tomb, which was finished and dedicated shortly after his death by his son and heir Chan-Bahlum.

The busy scribes and sculptors who decorated the House of Nine Images with column after column of Mayan hieroglyphs noted all the important events of Hanab-Pacal's reign, along with the reigns and death dates of the ten ahauob of Bak who came before him, and the major calendar cycles that rolled over during his reign. Hanab-Pacal's accession took place during the ninth katun of the ninth baktun, for example, and in standard Mayan style, the scribes linked that phase of the cycle of time to the enthronement of an ancestral god a little over 1,246,886 years beforehand. They also noted the date of Hanab-Pacal's own enthronement, 5 Lamat 1 Mol in the Mayan calendar, and referenced the actions of another deity on this date—which, like every date in the Mayan calendar cycle, repeats once every fifty-two years—when it had its eightieth repetition after Pacal's time on October 23, 4772, just eight days after the current piktun ends.

This is anything but an isolated example. Hundreds of Mayan inscriptions refer to dates after 2012, sometimes a few decades or centuries beyond it, sometimes a million years or more. Some authors influenced by the apocalypse meme have claimed that these future dates don't count, since they refer to mythical rather than historical dates, but of course the same argument applies just as well to December 21, 2012—the date, remember, when a Mayan god descends to some unknown destination. There's nothing at all to distinguish the 2012 date from the hundreds of other future dates in Mayan sources, except that it has become yet another temporary anchor for the apocalypse meme.

The inscriptions in the House of Nine Images seem to be saying, among other things, that Hanab-Pacal's fame will last beyond the end of the current cycle of time. They may be right. Now that the hieroglyphs have been deciphered, the fantasies that once cluttered up the legacy of the Maya have given way to a keen appreciation of a brilliant and innovative people who crafted one of the great civilizations of the ancient world, and whose descendants are still very much alive in the same regions of Central America today. Still, the old fantasies remain glued solidly in place in one corner of popular culture—the conviction, on the part of a great many people these days, that the ancient Mayans predicted the end of the world on December 21, 2012.

Ω

If the ancient Mayans didn't predict the end of the world in 2012, where did the prophecy come from? The answer adds richness to the irony, for the entire 2012 prophecy was invented out of whole cloth in the 1970s by two of the popular alternative thinkers of that time, Terence McKenna and José Argüellés.

McKenna belonged to that group of Sixties intellectuals who believed that psychedelic drugs were the key to higher dimensions of human consciousness. Unlike such relatively mainstream figures as Timothy Leary, though, McKenna went beyond the popular hallucinogens of the time to experiment with far more exotic compounds. Ayahuasca, a potent blend of two psychedelic plants used by shamans in the Amazon since time out of mind, was one of his favorites, and he took to combining ayahuasca with other drugs in an attempt to hallucinate his way to the higher reaches of human potential.

His theory about 2012 was the product of one of the resulting trips. While thoroughly stoned on a mix of ayahuasca and psychedelic mushrooms, he had a vision that included, among many other things, the idea that time was speeding up and would reach infinite speed sometime in the very near future, resulting in nothing less than the end of time itself. Later, his research into the *I Ching* convinced him that the sixty-four hexagrams of the ancient Chinese oracle encoded a hidden lunar calendar of 384 days, which is a little more than the number of days in thirteen lunar cycles.

Sixty-four of these cycles make a period of a little over sixty-seven years; sixty-four of these periods makes a longer cycle of 4,306 years, which is fairly close to the 4320 years taken up by two precessional ages; this process can be repeated until you reach a bit over seventy-two billion years, which McKenna decided was the total length of time the universe would exist. Since his drug vision convinced him that time was about to end, McKenna became convinced that there was only one sixty-seven-and-a-third-year cycle left to go. Like most of his generation, he considered the atomic bombing of Hiroshima on August 6, 1945, to be one of history's great turning points—it had much the same cachet in his time that September 11, 2001, has now—and counting ahead one cycle from there gave him November 17, 2012, as the date of the end of time. Later on, when he happened to read about the rollover of the Mayan calendar a little over a month later, he calmly adjusted his calculations to make his "Timewave Zero" end on that date.

The flurry of assumptions, approximations, and casual adjustments that went into the Timewave Zero theory don't exactly surround it with an aura of confidence, though it may be overly cynical to point out that this sort of "close enough" attitude was all too typical of the Sixties counterculture from which McKenna emerged. The Timewave Zero theory also involves fairly specific predictions of when bursts of "novelty"—unexpected or original events—ought to happen in the years between 1945 and 2010, and those predictions by and large haven't panned out. Still, this hasn't prevented believers in a 2012 apocalypse from citing

McKenna's theory as another bit of supporting evidence.

Far more influential than McKenna in launching the 2012 phenomenon, though, was José Argüellés. A leading light of the 1970s New Age movement and founding director of that decade's famous Whole Earth Festivals, Argüellés got into the apocalypse business in the run-up to the Harmonic Convergence of August 16, 1987. As mentioned in Chapter Five, it was Argüellés who coined the phrase "harmonic convergence," and his book *The Mayan Factor: Path Beyond Technology*—published just months before the Convergence—redefined the event in terms of the Mayan calendar, introducing December 21, 2012, to the collective conversation of our time.

In the wake of Argüellés's book, the Mayans became a hot property, and other writers were not slow to climb onto the bandwagon. One of the most interesting and readable of this second wave of 2012 speculators is John Major Jenkins, whose work has the added benefit—not shared by most other figures in the field—of drawing extensively on Mayan myth and the findings of archeology. Jenkins seems to have been the first to point out that at the winter solstice in 2012, the Sun will be aligned with the center of the Milky Way galaxy, and his theory is that this alignment, which he claims is prefigured in the architecture and city plan of the proto-Mayan site of Izapa, is the focal point of the entire Mayan mythology and calendrical cycle, and will usher in a dramatically new age of human consciousness.

Unfortunately, the evidence he cites to back this claim amounts to circular reasoning: in effect, he's successfully proved that if you start out with the assumption that the alignment of the solstice Sun and the galactic center is the basis for all Mayan myth and symbolism, you can find plenty of ways to support that claim. Thus the world tree on the richly carved stone lid on the tomb of Hanab-Pacal II in the House of Nine Images in Palenque, the head of an alligator on a stela in Izapa, and countless other bits of Mayan art become for Jenkins simply another set of emblems of the intersection of the ecliptic and the galactic core. It's rather reminiscent of those Freudians for whom everything longer than its width represents a penis.

What of the conjunction of the solstice Sun with the galactic core, though? Doesn't that prove that the Mayans thought that December 21, 2012, was a very important date? Not really. Because the galactic core fills a relatively broad section of space, and the movement of the Sun's solstice position through it creeps ahead at the glacial speed of precession, the conjunction actually first happened on the winter solstice of 1980 and will continue to happen every year until 2016—a period of almost two katunob, in Mayan terms—so the match is a good deal less impressive than it looks at first glance.

Other calendars pass through milestones of their own at intervals during that period, and ours is among them. Jenkins's own logic, in fact, could be applied just as easily to the Christian calendar, since on Christmas Day in the year 2000—exactly two millennia since that calendar began its count of time!—the Sun was exactly aligned with the galactic center. Just as Jenkins equates the cross-shaped

Mayan world tree emblem with the intersection of the ecliptic and the galactic center, the Christian cross could be interpreted as an emblem of the same thing, and the crucifixion of Jesus turned into a prophecy of some redemptive event or other scheduled to occur on December 25, 2000.

Nothing particular happened on that day, of course, and that's exactly the point. It's easy to come up with arguments to back the claim that the world will be transformed utterly on any given date, if you look hard enough, and the current crop of writers who have embraced December 21, 2012, as their apocalypse du jour can't possibly be accused of not looking hard enough. Thus Gregg Braden insists that we can expect the Earth's magnetic poles to reverse and the Sun to fling catastrophic solar flares our way in 2012; Peter Russell claims that the rate of evolutionary change will accelerate to infinity in 2012 and usher in a new "Wisdom Age"; Meg Blackburn Losey announces that electromagnetic radiations in 2012 will reawaken our DNA and cause a great leap forward in human evolution, and so on. It all looks very impressive until you notice that the only evidence being offered that any of these things are going to happen is that everybody knows that something's going to happen in 2012.

What all this means, of course, is simply that the apocalypse meme has found a new group of people to exploit. The same gaudy promises and bloodcurdling threats that have been trotted out at regular intervals since Zarathustra's time are being put through their paces again to ornament yet another claim that history as we know it is about to come to an screeching halt. In the wake of the Marxists and the Millerites, the Essenes and the Yellow Turbans, and all their equivalents across the last three millennia, today's believers in a 2012 apocalypse have let themselves be drawn into buying the comforting fantasy that the world around them will suddenly and cataclysmically be replaced by a new world more to their liking.

What will happen, in turn, on the morning of December 22, 2012, when the Sun rises as usual over a world that stubbornly refuses to follow the script and provide the believers with the Great Turning of their dreams? If the prediction catches fire in the collective conversation of today's culture, the result might be a Great Disappointment equal to that of 1844, a public humiliation drastic enough to drive today's New Age movement to the fringes of society for two or three generations. Equally, the prophets of the 2012 apocalypse might well simply find some new date further in the future and come up with a plausible reason why the new date makes more sense than the old.

One way or another, it's probably safe to assume that there will be plenty of apocalyptic prophecies littering the landscapes of the future with the wreckage of unborn generations' hopes and dreams—unless, that is, we step past today's glib talk about transformation and do something genuinely transformative.

Unless we confront the apocalypse meme itself.

AFTERWORD:

THE SEVENTH SEAL

When the seventh seal was opened, says the Book of Revelation, there was silence in heaven for the space of half an hour. In a very real sense, that brief interval of expectation in total stillness sums up the whole history of the apocalypse meme. For more than three thousand years now, people have managed to convince themselves that their world was teetering on the brink of total transformation, that their enemies were about to be annihilated and their own fondest hopes fulfilled by a shattering event that would change the nature of reality itself. For more than three thousand years, they have waited in breathless anticipation, moment by moment, for the great change to manifest.

That sense of overwhelming immediacy is the bait dangled by the apocalypse meme, the thing that keeps people hooked on apocalyptic dreams even when every scrap of evidence, not to mention common sense, points in the other direction. It's easy to show this by a counterexample. According to Daniel 8:14, the text that sent William Miller on the long road to the Great Disappointment, "the sanctuary shall be cleansed" 2300 days after the destruction of the Temple of Solomon by the Babylonians; according to 2 Peter 3:8, "one day of the Lord is as a thousand years." One very reasonable interpretation is that the Second Coming will occur 2300 "days" of a thousand years each after the destruction of the Temple, which will put the Second Coming right on time in the year 2,299,414 CE— in other words, more than two million years from now. That date provides an obvious, literal meaning of those two passages, and nothing in Scripture contradicts it—if Jesus can say "Behold, I come quickly," and then wait two thousand years, he can just as easily wait two million—but it has been studiously avoided by every prophet of Christian apocalypse from Bishop Hilarian to Tim LaHaye, because it deprives the believer in apocalypse of one of the powerful emotional payoffs that drives the meme.

Understand those payoffs and you understand the meme itself. When it comes right down to it, after all, the vast majority of people who insist that they believe in the imminent fulfillment of some apocalyptic prophecy don't actually live in accordance with that belief. How many of the millions of people nowadays who insist that a new golden age of universal enlightenment and abundance will arrive in 2012, or who treat it as a given that the Rapture will occur during their lifetimes, have stopped putting money into their retirement accounts? More generally, how many people down through the centuries have actually lived their lives as though the world was about to end? From Zarathustra through Jan Bockelson to Marshall Applewhite and his followers, lying dead in their San Diego mansion while Comet Hale-Bopp soared through the skies above them, there have always been a few, but in nearly every case those few have embraced the logical consequences of their beliefs only after circumstances or their own dubious choices have closed off every other possibility.

It's the emotional payoffs of apocalyptic faith here and now, rather, that explain the extraordinary persistence of the meme over more than three thousand years of history. The payoffs are not always the same from case to case. To true believers, whether their belief fixates on a religious doctrine or a secular one, the apocalypse meme promises a future in which they will be proved right and everyone who disagrees with them will be forced to admit the error of their ways; to the idealistic, the arrival of a world more perfect than human arrangements have ever been able to provide; to the frustrated, the resentful, and the angry, a settling of scores on a superhumanly grandiose scale. Like the magic jewel in a fairy tale that makes everyone think they are seeing whatever they most desire, the apocalypse meme promises all things to all people. The one common feature to the wild diversity of its promises is the hope of a sudden, total, and permanent end to the dissatisfactions that are inseparable from life in the real world.

One night over a pleasant dinner of takeout Thai food, a friend of mine, a spiritual teacher of many years' experience, recounted a story that sums up this core dimension of the apocalypse meme. In the last months of 1999, he happened to meet a woman who said that she was profoundly worried about the Y2K problem. He thought, reasonably enough, that what worried her was the prospect of cascading computer failures causing power grids and the banking system to seize up, potentially causing worldwide chaos, but she quickly set him straight. Her life was unsatisfying, her career was going nowhere, her marriage was on the rocks; what worried her was the possibility that on the morning of January 1, 2000, she would wake up and have to deal with the same painfully mundane realities that she'd had to confront the day before.

The seductive promise of the apocalypse meme is precisely that it seems to offer a free ticket out of the troubles of everyday life, whether those are as petty as the ones that afflicted the woman in my friend's narrative, or as bitter and insoluble as those that drove the Lakota in 1889 and 1890 to take up the Ghost Dance. During that half hour of silence in heaven, when the prophecy has been uttered but not yet put to the test, the meme very often brings to those who embrace it an intoxicating sense of freedom; the imagined presence of the shining new world about to dawn makes it easy to let go of every kind of fear and emotional burden. The downside, though, arrives just as soon as the prophecy is put to the test, for the apocalypse meme has another constant feature: the predictions it generates are always wrong.

Ω

Put thus baldly, that last comment will likely rouse the ire of believers in those apocalyptic prophecies that haven't yet been put to the test by events, and may raise reasonable questions in the minds of people who don't happen to believe in any particular apocalypse, but like to keep an open mind about the future. How can anyone be absolutely sure that not one of the hundreds of apocalyptic prophecies currently in circulation will ever come true?

To answer that question, it's important to be clear about what exactly counts as an apocalyptic prophecy. It's not enough to predict that something bad will happen to a community, or a country, or the whole world, or that some unexpected good will come to a group of people who are disadvantaged in some way. Such predictions do get made fairly often, and it's a matter of historical record that some of them come true; when a few thoughtful observers of the international scene worried in the years before 1914 that the great powers of Europe might blunder into a catastrophic war, for example, or when the most optimistic American feminists in the 1830s dreamed that a day might come when women would be able to vote, they were quite correct to say as much.

Notice, though, that neither of these predictions required

the laws of nature, the realities of human existence, and the ordinary workings of society to come to a screeching halt. It's precisely this latter fantasy that forms the throbbing heart of the apocalypse meme: the promise that life as we know it, with all its frustrations, limitations, and annoyances, will be replaced by something wholly other—something that normally just happens to correspond to whatever the fondest fantasies of its believers happens to be. Human nature being what it is, those fantasies inevitably include a good-sized helping of the impossible, whether that takes the form of eternal bliss in a world transformed into paradise, as it does in so many religious apocalypses, or the slightly less blatantly supernatural promise of perfect peace, harmony, and prosperity forever, as it does in secular apocalypses of the Marxist sort.

The apocalypse meme, in other words, encourages people to believe in promises of a kind that will never be fulfilled. In this, it has much in common with another meme that's had a very thorough workout in recent decades—the meme that drives speculative bubbles. Those readers who were paying attention during the real estate bubble that crashed and burned in 2008 already know a fair amount about that meme, but they may not realize that every feature of the recent boom and bust can be tracked in identical booms and busts reaching back through history to the first recorded example of the type, the Dutch tulip mania that bubbled and burst in 1637.

The story of the tulip mania is worth recounting, as it's as good an example of the speculative bubble meme as any. Tulips had been a popular flower in Dutch gardens and window boxes for years beforehand, but in the decade or so before 1637, buoyed by an expanding economy, the market for exotic tulips began to grow steadily. Tulip merchants started to make serious money, and people outside the tulip trade began to dabble in tulip futures in the simple ways that were available at the time, which mostly consisted of buying tulip bulbs they thought would go up in price and selling them later for whatever profit they could get.

By 1636, as a result, the prices of tulip bulbs soared steadily upwards, and substantial amounts of money were being made, by those who bought and sold them. Few people involved in the tulip trade were dabbling by that point. Instead, much of the Netherlands came to be convinced that tulip bulbs would go up in price indefinitely, and anyone who went long on tulips could get very, very rich. More people duly got into the market, and the price of tulip bulbs soared to stratospheric levels. Tulip speculators quit their day jobs to buy and sell tulips full time; on the streets, in the coffeehouses, at social gatherings, nobody talked about anything else; huge fortunes were made, lost, and made again.

Then, as with every other speculative bubble, reality reasserted itself. On March 2, 1637, the tulip market crashed. To the horror of investors who had their entire net worth and more in the tulip market, the tulip bulbs they had bought at fantastically inflated prices suddenly started losing ground. Despite all efforts to prop up the market and convince people that tulips would return to their former prices, the bubble was over, and by the time tulip bulbs had finished transitioning back from hot investment property to pretty flower, thousands of people across the Netherlands had lost everything they had.

Replace tulips with tech stocks, subprime real estate, credit default swaps, or any other investment opportunity that's been through the cycle of boom and bust, and it's a familiar story. In each of these cases, and every other example of a speculative bubble, people convinced themselves that the price of whatever investment was at the center of the bubble could keep on rising indefinitely. That sort of thinking becomes a self-fulfilling prophecy—rising prices attract new investors to the market, and money from the new investors drives prices up even further—but sooner or later the supply of new investors runs out, prices begin to slide, investors start to pull their money out, and panic sets in. The only question at that point is just how much economic damage will be done by the time the last of the rubble stops bouncing.

The pattern is utterly predictable, the meme impossible to miss, and most of the rhetoric is supplied by the meme in advance, word for word. When the real estate boom of 2005 and 2006 was in full roar, the same slogans that had been trotted out by stock promoters to justify the stock market excesses of 1929—and thus found their way into John Kenneth Galbraith's wry chronicle *The Great Crash 1929*—were trotted out again, often in identical words, by real estate promoters. Those same slogans will be used again, and they will be just as mistaken then, too.

When a friend comes up to you at a party five or ten

years from now, in other words, and insists that whatever speculative asset happens to be popular at that time really can keep on increasing in price for decades to come, your friend is wrong. You don't have to know a thing about the asset, or the market it's traded in, or any other of the details your friend is eager to tell you; once you learn to recognize the bubble meme—the delusion that an asset that's rising in price because of pure crowd psychology will keep on rising in price forever—you know that a crash is coming, because that's how the bubble meme always plays out.

In exactly the same way, if a friend comes up to you and insists that the world as we know it is about to be replaced by something that bears a suspicious resemblance to the hopes, fears, and fantasies of some corner of today's popular culture, whether the excuse for the claim is the Rapture, the Singularity, the assortment of transformations currently pinned onto the end of the thirteenth baktun of the Mayan calendar, or what have you, your friend is wrong: as wrong as Thomas Müntzer, William Miller, Nostradamus, Dorothy Martin, and all the other people down through the centuries who have allowed the apocalypse meme to do their thinking for them, who waited breathlessly for the world to end, and who found out the hard way that the world is under no obligation to conform to human fantasies.

Ω

Someday far in the future—about four billion years from now, according to current astrophysical theory—the core of the Sun will have burnt enough of its hydrogen fuel that it can no longer counter the pressure of its own gravity. As it gradually collapses inwards, over the next two billion years, the Sun will balloon into a red giant, a hundred times larger than it is today, and any life that happens to remain on Earth at that distant date will be crisped by daytime temperatures that will peak somewhere around 2600° F. A quarter million years or so later, the Sun's core will pass a critical threshold and start fusing helium; the resulting "helium flash" will blast a third of the Sun's mass into deep space in a matter of minutes. In all probability, whatever charred cinder remains of the Earth at that point will be blown to smithereens by that blast, and its fragments will be scattered back into the interstellar dust from which it formed some ten billion years before.

Countless millions of years before that happens, it's a safe bet that humanity will have gone extinct. The average species, according to the few available rough estimates, lasts for about a million years, and our species, *Homo sapiens*, has existed for around two hundred thousand years, or something like a fifth of that theoretical span; the average genus, again according to a rough estimate, lasts for about ten million years, and our genus, *Homo*, has been around for maybe a quarter of that. All of recorded history amounts to five thousand years so far, so if our species has an average lifespan and maintains written records from now on, we have compiled a little more than half of one percent of our ultimate written history. Still, one way or another, the time will doubtless come when the last human beings die out, possibly to be replaced after a time by some other intelligent species, perhaps not.

Much closer to our own time, in all probability, our current civilization will have joined the long list of human societies that overshot their resource base and ended up as one more addition to history's compost heap. One common fantasy these days insists that contemporary industrial civilization has nothing in common with the civilizations of the past, and thus can expect to soar endlessly upwards to some date with destiny out there among the stars; another common fantasy insists with equal fervor that contemporary industrial civilization is poised on the brink of cataclysm and will shortly and suddenly be annihilated for its sins. Both of these fantasies come straight out of the apocalypse meme, one by way of Joachim of Fiore and the Marquis de Condorcet, the other by way of secular rehashings of the standard Christian apocalyptic myth, and both can therefore be discounted. It's far more likely that future generations will visit the crumbling remains of today's urban centers the way we visit the ruined cities of Egypt and the ancient Mayans, and scholars of that distant time will argue with one another about the reasons why the ancient Americans traced out the same course of political dysfunction, economic decline, and eventual technological collapse as so many other civilizations before—and, no doubt, since.

These three predictions, speculative as they inevitably must be, share a common theme: in the real world, everything eventually comes to an end. Worlds perish in stellar fire, species go extinct, civilizations decline and fall, and of course each one of us inhabits a body that is ripening toward death with every moment that passes, and will eventually do what it was born to do and shut down. In one of its most important senses, the apocalypse meme is a response to the awareness of these hard facts—or, more precisely, it's an evasion of those facts, an attempt to pretend that they don't apply to us.

Thus it's wildly inaccurate to do as a surprisingly large number of writers about apocalyptic beliefs have done, and suggest that since the world will eventually come to an end, believers in an imminent apocalypse aren't entirely wrong. The apocalypse meme is not really about the end of the world, or more precisely, it's not about the kind of end that the world, or humanity, or contemporary industrial civilization, or each of our lives, will actually have. At the center of the apocalypse meme is the insistence that those endings aren't for us—that, as Joseph Rutherford insisted, millions now living will never die. It's worth remembering, though, that Rutherford did in fact die, and so did the millions to whom he promised eternal life; and so did the millions upon millions of others who expected to see the sky torn open and time shudder to a stop for their benefit, down through the centuries since Zarathustra first dreamed that the great wheel of time would stop turning; and so will I, and so, dear reader, will you.

It's been said, and rightly so, that the simple awareness of that last fact is the starting point of all human wisdom, or perhaps simply of that basic maturity which distinguishes the adult from the overgrown child. That wisdom, or that level of maturity, is badly needed just now. Our industrial civilization is in trouble; many of our nations and communities are facing severe problems; it's anyone's guess at this point whether there are any meaningful solutions left to the crises that beset us, or whether the best we can manage is to lessen the impact of those crises and salvage as much as possible from the wreckage as things come gradually apart. The one thing that can be said for certain is that waiting for a miracle to bail us out from the consequences of our own mismanagement—whether that miracle is marked by the end of the Mayan calendar, the coming of the Rapture, or any other excuse for the intoxicating folly of the apocalypse meme—isn't a meaningful response to the challenges of our time.

That doubtless won't stop plenty of people from turning to apocalyptic fantasies in the years to come. Still, the Great Disappointment convinced a great many Americans from the 1840s on that hope for the future had to be found in constructive action in the world rather than in fantasies that a supernatural event would hand them the world they desired, and some of the more colorful disasters launched by the apocalypse meme in previous centuries inspired similar reactions. In the same way, there's at least a chance that the upcoming failure of the 2012 prophecy might encourage people to take a hard and skeptical look at the apocalypse meme itself, to recognize that longing for the annihilation of most of humanity has no place in an authentic spirituality, and accept that our happiness as human beings depends on how we choose to live our lives here and now, in this beautiful world on which we each dance for so brief and precious a time. If the coming of 4 Ahau 3 Kankin 13.0.0.0.0 helps any significant number of people to reach that realization, then in its own way, it may actually bring a new era of enlightenment.

NOTES AND SOURCES

All quotations from the Bible are taken from the King James Version, cited by book, chapter, and verse.

FOREWORD:

Reingold and Dershowitz 2001 is the source for the alternative dates cited at the beginning of the Foreword.

CHAPTER ONE:

For the archaic stellar mythology and the myths of precession, see de Santillana and von Dechend 1977. The discussion of Zarathustra's pivotal role in the origins of the apocalypse meme is based on Norman Cohn's acute analysis in Cohn 1993; for a more general view of the Zoroastrian faith, see Zaehner 1961. For the problem of evil in polytheist and monotheist faiths, see Greer 2005.

For Chang Taoling and the millennarian origins of religious Taoism, see Schipper 1993. For a detailed study of a later Chinese apocalyptic rebellion, see Naquin 1976.

CHAPTER TWO:

Cohn 1993 is a principal source for the material in this chapter, especially for the gradual evolution of Jewish monotheism and the crucial borrowings of Zoroastrian ideas that made modern Judaism what it is. For the role of apocalyptic in the Maccabean revolt, see also Kirsch 2006, pp. 19–52. For the finding of the Dead Sea Scrolls and the most readable of the current English translations, see Wise, et al. 1996, the passage from the War Scroll is on p.152.

The Jewish revolt of 66–70 CE is chronicled in Faulkner 2004; the career of Flavius Josephus, whose account of the revolt remains the most important documentary source, is the subject of Rajak 1983.

For Sabbatai Zevi and the messianic movement that formed around him, Scholem 1976 is the classic study.

CHAPTER THREE:

The apocalyptic prophecy of Jesus cited here is summarized from Matthew 24:1-24; that of John is of course from the Book of Revelation. For the Gospel of Thomas, see Davies 1983; for Meyer's support, see Barnstone and Meyer 2003, pp. 31–42. For the mythology surrounding the year

1000, see McGinn 1979, pp. 88–90.

The origins of the belief in Earth's six-thousand-year history, and the varying views of Hilarian and Sulpicius Severus, are discussed in McGinn 1979, pp. 52–53. The prophecies of Beatus of Liébana are presented in McGinn, pp. 77–79, while the apocalyptic dimensions of the quarrel between Popes and Emperors are recounted in McGinn, pp. 94–102 and 168–179.

Adso of Melk's *Letter on the Antichrist* is discussed and excerpted in McGinn, pp. 82–87. For the Last Emperor, see McGinn, pp. 43–49, 70–76, and 85. For the Angelic Pope, see McGinn, pp. 186–195. Joachim of Flores is discussed in McGinn 1979, pp. 126–141. The Joachimist movement is covered in Cohn 1970, pp. 108–126, and McGinn, pp. 158–167; the Spiritual Franciscans in McGinn, pp. 203–217; and Fra Dolcino and the Apostolic Brethren in McGinn, pp. 226–229. For the heresy of the Free Spirit, see especially Cohn, pp. 148–186.

Hussite apocalyptic is discussed in Cohn, pp. 205–222, and McGinn, pp. 259–269. For Thomas Müntzer and the Peasants' War, see Cohn, pp. 234–250, and for the Münster revolt and the messianic reign of Jan Bockelson, see Cohn, pp. 261–280. A classic overview of the radical end of Reformation thought may be found in Williams 1962.

CHAPTER FOUR:

The best guide to the radical groups of the English Civil War era remains Hill 1984. The strange careers of Richard Brothers and Joanna Southcott are chronicled in Harrison

1979. For the Taiping Heavenly Kingdom, see Spence 1996. For the Mahdi of the Sudan, a good source is Pakenham 1991, especially pp. 259–275. For the Ghost Dance, Mooney 1896 is a contemporary report, while Brown 1970, pp. 415–450, provides an evocative account.

For the history of the secular faith in revolution from its origins in prerevolutionary France through the Carbonari and Marxism to its consummation in the Russian Revolution, Billington 1980 is a solid introduction. Charles Fourier's work is usefully outlined in Beecher 1986, and his impact on American thinking is explored in Guarneri 1991. Those of my readers who feel ready to cope with Hegel's theory of history will find a clear presentation in McCarney 2000.

CHAPTER FIVE:

For the Burned-Over District and the early days of American apocalypticism, see Barkun 1986. The Millerite movement has been chronicled from opposing points of view in Sears 1924 (from the critical side) and volume 4 of Froom 1954. See also Numbers and Butler 1987, an extremely useful anthology of papers covering many aspects of the movement. The quotation concerning Miller's orthodoxy is from Cross 1950, p. 320. The most colorful of the Millerite posters, published by Joshua V. Himes in 1843, has been reproduced in its original size as an insert to Numbers and Butler 1987.

For the history of Dispensationalism given here, see Boyer 1992, pp. 80–112. For the Pope as the Antichrist in

Pentecost and Lindsey, see Boyer, pp. 274–5, and Lindsey 1973. For Hitler and Mussolini as the Antichrist, see Boyer, pp. 108–9. For Sadat and Saddam Hussein as the Antichrist, see Boyer, pp. 275–6. For Gorbachev as the Antichrist, see Boyer, pp. 177–179. For David Wilkerson's opposing view, see Wilkerson 1998; the quotation is from p. 96.

For the UFO phenomenon, see Greer 2009; the story of the Dorothy Martin group is best read in Festinger 1964. The Singularity myth in all its lushness may be found in Kurzweil 2005.

The prophecies of Nostradamus may be found in Roberts 1994, among many other sources. Edward Kennedy's presidency is predicted on pages 210 and 218. The depopulation of Europe by floods is on page 7, and the Great King of Terror is prophesied on page 336; I have made my own translation of the French text here.

For the Harmonic Convergence, see Shearer 1975, Arguelles 1987, and Heley 2009, pp. 49–60.

CHAPTER SIX:

For Thompson's view of the ancient Maya, see Thompson 1954; for his role in the history of Mayan studies, and for the decipherment of the Mayan hieroglyphs, see Coe 1999. Proskouriakoff 1993 is a useful study of Mayan inscriptions as historical sources. For a good survey of the Maya as they are known from their own writings, see Schele and Mathews 1998.

For the Tortuguero inscription, see Heley 2009, p. 34. For the inscriptions in the House of Nine Images (Temple of Inscriptions, Palenque), see Schele and Mathews 1998, pp. 106–107. For claims that all post-2012 Mayan prophecies reference mythical rather than actual time, see Heley 2009, p. 8.

For the origins of McKenna's "Timewave Zero" theory, see McKenna 1994a; for the developed theory, see Heley 2009, pp. 123–131 and McKenna 1994b. For Argüellés's role in the creation of the 2012 phenomenon, see Arguelles 1987. For Thompson's lingering presence in New Age circles, see, for example, the bibliography of Heley 2009. For Jenkins, Braden, Russell, Losey, and a good general overview of the 2012 phenomenon, see Simon 2007.

AFTERWORD:

The best recent introduction to the speculative bubble meme is Reinhart and Rogoff 2009, though no student of the subject should miss the wry brilliance of Galbraith 1954. The classic study of the Dutch tulip bubble is still Mackay 1842.

BIBLIOGRAPHY

Argüellés, José. *The Mayan Factor: Path Beyond Technology.* Santa Fe, NM: Bear & Company, 1987.

Barkun, Michael. *Crucible of the Millennium: The Burned-Over District of New York in the 1840s.* Syracuse, NY: Syracuse University Press, 1986.

Barnstone, Willis, and Marvin Meyer. *The Gnostic Bible.* Boston: Shambhala, 2003.

Beecher, Jonathan. *Charles Fourier: The Visionary and his World.* Berkeley: University of California Press, 1986.

Billington, James H. *Fire in the Minds of Men: Origins of the Revolutionary Faith.* New York: Transaction, 1980.

Boyer, Paul. *When Time Shall Be No More: Prophecy Belief in Modern American Culture.* Cambridge, MA: Harvard University Press, 1992.

Brown, Dee. *Bury My Heart at Wounded Knee*. New York: Holt, Rinehart and Winston, 1970.

Browne, Sylvia. *End of Days: Predictions and Prophecies About the End of the World*. New York: Dutton, 2008.

Coe, Michael D. *Breaking the Maya Code*. New York: Thames and Hudson, 1999.

Cohn, Norman. *Chaos, Cosmos and the World to Come: The Ancient Roots of Apocalyptic Faith*. New Haven, CT: Yale University Press, 1993.

———. *The Pursuit of the Millennium*. Oxford: Oxford University Press, 1970.

Cross, Whitney R. *The Burned-Over District*. Ithaca, NY: Cornell University Press, 1950.

Davies, Stevan L. *The Gospel of Thomas and Christian Wisdom*. New York: Seabury, 1983.

de Santillana, Giorgio de, and Hertha von Dechend. *Hamlet's Mill: An Essay on Myth and the Frame of Time*. Boston: Nonpareil Books, 1977.

Faulkner, Neil. *Apocalypse: The Great Jewish Revolt Against Rome*. Stroud, Gloucestershire: Tempus Publishing, 2004.

Festinger, Leon, Henry W. Riecken, and Stanley Schachter. *When Prophecy Fails*. New York: Harper & Row, 1964.

Froom, Leroy. *The Prophetic Faith of our Fathers*, Vol. 4. Washington, DC: Review and Herald Publishing Association, 1954.

Galbraith, John Kenneth. *The Great Crash 1929*. Boston: Houghton Mifflin, 1954.

Greer, John Michael. *A World Full of Gods: An Inquiry into Polytheism*. Tucson, AZ: ADF Press, 2005.

———. *The UFO Phenomenon: Fact, Fantasy, and Disinformation*. Woodbury, MN: Llewellyn, 2009.

Guarneri, Carl J. *The Utopian Alternative: Fourierism in Nineteenth-Century America*. Ithaca, NY: Cornell University Press, 1991.

Harrison, J. F. C. *The Second Coming: Popular Millenarianism, 1780–1850*. New Brunswick. NJ: Rutgers University Press, 1979.

Heley, Mark. *The Everything Guide to 2012*. Avon, MA: Adams Media, 2009.

Hill, Christopher. *The World Turned Upside Down: Radical Ideas during the English Revolution*. London: Penguin, 1984.

Kirsch, Jonathan. *A History of the End of the World*. San Francisco: HarperOne, 2006.

Kurzweil, Ray. *The Singularity is Near*. New York: Viking, 2005.

LaHaye, Tim, and Thomas Ice. *Charting the End Times*. Eugene, OR: Harvest House, 2001.

Licón, Ernesto González. *Vanished American Civilizations: The History and Cultures of the Zapotecs and Mixtecs*. Translated by Andrew Ellis. Armonk, NY: Sharpe, 2001.

Lindsey, Hal. *The Late Great Planet Earth*. New York: Bantam Books, 1973.

Love, Bruce. *The Paris Codex: Handbook for a Maya Priest*. Austin: University of Texas Press, 1994.

Mackay, Charles. *Extraordinary Popular Delusions and the Madness of Crowds*. London: National Illustrated Library, 1842.

McCarney, Joe. *Routledge Philosophy Guidebook to Hegel on History*. London: Routledge, 2000.

McGinn, Bernard. *Visions of the End: Apocalyptic Traditions in the Middle Ages*. New York: Columbia University Press, 1979.

McKenna, Terence. *The Invisible Landscape: Mind, Hallucinogens, and the I Ching.* San Francisco: HarperOne, 1994; cited as McKenna 1994a.

————. *True Hallucinations.* San Francisco: HarperOne, 1994; cited as McKenna 1994b.

Mooney, James. *The Ghost-Dance Religion and Wounded Knee.* 1896 original; reprint New York: Dover, 1973.

Naquin, Susan. *Millennarian Rebellion in China: The Eight Trigrams Uprising of 1913.* New Haven, CT: Yale University Press, 1976.

Numbers, Ronald L., and Jonathan M. Butler, eds. *The Disappointed: Millerism and Millenarianism in the Nineteenth Century.* Bloomington, IN: Indiana University Press, 1987.

Pakenham, Thomas. *The Scramble for Africa: White Man's Conquest of the Dark Continent from 1876 to 1912.* New York: HarperCollins, 1991.

Proskouriakoff, Tatiana. *Maya History.* Austin: University of Texas Press, 1993.

Rajak, Tessa. *Josephus: The Historian and his Society.* London: Duckworth, 1983.

Reingold, Edward M., and Nachum Dershowitz. *Calendrical Calculations.* Cambridge: Cambridge University Press, 2001.

Reinhart, Carmen M., and Kenneth S. Rogoff. *This Time is Different: Eight Centuries of Financial Folly.* Princeton, NJ: Princeton University Press, 2009.

Roberts, Henry C. *The Complete Prophecies of Nostradamus.* New York: Crown, 1994.

Roys, Ralph L., trans. and ed. *The Book of Chilam Balam of Chumayel.* Norman, OK: University of Oklahoma Press, 1967.

Schele, Linda, and David Friedel. *A Forest of Kings: The An-*

cient Maya Revealed. New York: Morrow, 1990.

Schele, Linda, and Peter Mathews. *The Code of Kings*. New York: Scribner, 1998.

Schipper, Kristofer. *The Taoist Body*. Translated by Karen C. Duval. Berkeley: University of California Press, 1993.

Scholem, Gershom. *Sabbatai Sevi, the Mystical Messiah*. Translated by R. J. Zwi Werblowski. Princeton, NJ: Princeton University Press, 1976.

Sears, Clara Endicott. *Days of Delusion: A Strange Bit of History*. Boston: Houghton Mifflin, 1924.

Shearer, Tony. *Beneath the Moon and Under the Sun*. Houston, TX: Sun Publishing, 1975.

Simon, Tami, ed. *The Mystery of 2012: Predictions, Prophecies, and Possibilities*. Boulder, CO: Sounds True, 2007.

Spence, Jonathan D. *God's Chinese Son: The Taiping Heavenly Kingdom of Hong Xiuquan*. New York: W.W. Norton, 1996.

Stanton, E. F. *Christ and Other Klansmen, or, Lives of Love*. Kansas City, MS: Harper and Stanton, 1924.

Thompson, J. Eric S. *The Rise and Fall of Maya Civilization*. Norman, OK: University of Oklahoma Press, 1954.

Thrupp, Sylvia L., ed. *Millennial Dreams in Action: Studies in Revolutionary Religious Movements*. New York: Schocken Books, 1970.

Wilkerson, David. *God's Plan to Protect His People in the Coming Depression*. Lindale, TX: Wilkerson Trust, 1998.

Williams, George. *The Radical Reformation*. Philadelphia: Westminster Press, 1962.

Wise, Michael, Martin Abegg, Jr., and Edward Cook. *The Dead Sea Scrolls: A New Translation*. San Francisco: HarperOne, 1996.

Zaehner, R. C. *The Dawn and Twilight of Zoroastrianism*. New York: G.P. Putnam's Sons, 1961.

INDEX

ABOUT THE AUTHOR

Born in the gritty Navy town of Bremerton, Washington, and raised in Seattle's suburbs, JOHN MICHAEL GREER started to write about the time he could first hold a pencil. The author, to date, of twenty-seven nonfiction books and one science fiction novel, he also writes The Archdruid Report, a weekly blog on peak oil and the future of industrial society, and serves as the presiding officer of a contemporary Druid order, the Ancient Order of Druids in America. He currently lives in the mountains of western Maryland with his wife Sara.

TO OUR READERS

Viva Editions publishes books that inform, enlighten, and entertain. We do our best to bring you, the reader, quality books that celebrate life, inspire the mind, revive the spirit, and enhance lives all around. Our authors are practical visionaries: people who offer deep wisdom in a hopeful and helpful manner. Viva was launched with an attitude of growth and we want to spread our joy and offer our support and advice where we can to help you live the Viva way: vivaciously!

We're grateful for all our readers and want to keep bringing you books for inspired living. We invite you to write to us with your comments and suggestions, and what you'd like to see more of. You can also sign up for our online newsletter to learn about new titles, author events, and special offers.

Viva Editions
2246 Sixth St.
Berkeley, CA 94710
www.vivaeditions.com
(800) 780-2279
Follow us on Twitter @vivaeditions
Friend/fan us on Facebook